Twayne's United States Authors Series

Sylvia E. Bowman, *Editor*

INDIANA UNIVERSITY

Bayard Taylor

Bayard Taylor

By PAUL C. WERMUTH
Northeastern University

 228

Twayne Publishers, Inc.   ::   New York

To the Memory of
My Father,
Paul Charles Wermuth

Preface

BAYARD TAYLOR was a cultural phenomenon of considerable interest and significance. His popularity during most of his life was little short of remarkable; and any writer who is that widely read attracts our attention and our questions. Of course, his fame came mostly from his travels and his lectures; but he was also widely known as a poet, novelist, translator, critic, and so forth. It would be interesting to know what qualities in his work were attractive to so many people; what that can tell us about the taste of those people and of that time; why his reputation declined so drastically; and what is the relationship between an author's own taste and his popular success.

A basic question concerns Taylor's almost total disappearance from the literary scene since his death in 1878. Did those who admired his work simply have bad taste? Was his reputation artificially created by manipulation of the literary world? Has literary taste changed so drastically? It should be remembered that Taylor was more popular and more widely admired than, say, Walt Whitman—and not only by the public at large but also by responsible literary men. As for what led to such a gross misjudgment, if such it was, the answers to these questions may lie in the American experience in the nineteenth century, in the conditions of making a living in America, or in the social system. I think some of them, at least, lie in that cluster of attitudes, beliefs, and ideas we call the "Genteel Tradition," which is related to but not identical with English Victorianism. Taylor was, without much doubt, one of the best embodiments of that tradition, as I hope this volume will show. It is perhaps this very representativeness that catches one's interest; for Taylor, it seems to me, was The Writer in nineteenth-century America, and the ways he was aided and hampered by the Genteel Tradition is the burden of this study.

This book is largely a study of Taylor's published works rather than of his life, though some biographical material is, of course, unavoidable. A good deal of the book is necessarily paraphrase and summary; but I hope that an accurate description and a sensible evaluation of his work may suggest some answers to the questions raised above, though obviously, the reader may arrive at different conclusions than those presented here. One chief problem in dealing with Taylor is the sheer mass of material; for, not only did he publish some fifty volumes, but there are some twenty thousand of his letters extant; and the quantity of his uncollected periodical contributions is staggering. In handling this mass of material, selection has been necessary; but, for the most part, I have tried to let Taylor himself talk as much as possible. The talking he does here is, I think, accurate and representative.

Paul C. Wermuth

Boston, Massachusetts
1971

Acknowledgments

Thanks are due to many libraries for permission to use their resources—Yale, Trinity (of Hartford), Harvard, and others. There is also supposed to be a large body of Taylor material in the hands of a private collector in Pennsylvania, but its contents can only be guessed. Thanks are due, also, to Central Connecticut State College for a sabbatical leave which helped me to finish this study. And finally, my wife, Barbara, must be thanked for her steady and perceptive help all the way through.

Contents

Chronology

1825   Bayard Taylor born in village of Kennett Square, Chester County, Pennsylvania, on January 11. Fourth child (first to live to maturity) of Joseph and Rebecca (Way) Taylor. Family mostly English Quakers, though both grandmothers were South Germans. Named for James A. Bayard, a Delaware senator.

1829   Family moved to farm one mile from Kennett Square.

1837   Father elected county sheriff; family moved to West Chester for three years. Attended Bolmar's Academy.

1840   First publication: account of a visit to Brandywine battlefield, published in *West Chester Register*.

1841   First poem published, in *The Saturday Evening Post* of Philadelphia: "Soliloquy of a Young Poet."

1842   Formal education ended in academy at Unionville, where he also taught briefly.

1842   Apprenticed for four years to a printer in West Chester. Made one of his earliest literary connections by writing to Rufus Griswold, who encouraged him.

1844   Published (by subscription) *Ximena; or The Battle of the Sierra Morena & Other Poems*, dedicated to Rufus Griswold. In July, sailed for Liverpool to begin a two-year trip through Europe.

1846   Shortly after return, published *Views A-Foot*, which became a best seller, with six editions its first year. Made trip to Boston to meet New England worthies. With F. E. Foster, bought a Phoenixville, Pennsylvania, newspaper; and issued first number of *The Pioneer* on December 29, 1846.

1847   Gave up newspaper after one year; went to New York to enter literary world.

1848   Began lifelong association with Horace Greeley's *Tribune*. *Rhymes of Travel, Ballads, and Poems* published.

1849   Ninth edition of *Views A-Foot*. Sent to California by the *Tribune* to report on gold rush.

1850   Published *El Dorado; or Adventures in the Path of Empire*. Delivered Phi Beta Kappa poem at Harvard Commencement. Married childhood sweetheart, Mary Agnew, who died shortly after.

1851   *A Book of Romances, Lyrics, and Songs*.

1851- Trip to Near and Far East; accompanied Commodore Perry's
1853   expedition to Japan.

1854   Returned home, began lecturing. *A Journey to Central Africa;
       The Land of the Saracens; Poems of the Orient.*

1855   *A Visit to India, China, & Japan in the Year 1853; Poems of
       Home and Travel.*

1856   *Cyclopaedia of Modern Travel.*

1857   Married Marie Hansen, daughter of a German astronomer;
       Northern Travel.

1858   Daughter Lilian born.

1859   California lecture tour; published *Travels in Greece and
       Russia; At Home and Abroad,* first series.

1860   Finished building "Cedarcroft," his mansion at Kennett Square.

1862   Appointed secretary of legation, then chargé d'affaires at St.
       Petersburg, Russia; resigned in 1863. *The Poet's Journal;
       At Home and Abroad,* Second Series.

1863   Brother Fred killed at Gettysburg. *Hannah Thurston: A Story
       of American Life.*

1864   *Poems of Bayard Taylor* (Blue & Gold edition); *John God-
       frey's Fortunes.*

1866   *The Story of Kennett; The Picture of St. John.*

1868   *The Golden Wedding: A Masque.*

1869   Ode on dedication of monument at Gettysburg. Dedicated
       statue of Fitz-Greene Halleck at Guilford, Connecticut. Ac-
       cepted nonresident professorship of German literature at Cor-
       nell. Monthly column for *Putnam's Magazine* on foreign
       literature and art. Reviewed poetry for the *Tribune. By-Ways
       of Europe.*

1870   Lectured at Cornell University on German literature. Second
       California lecture trip. *Faust,* Part I; *Joseph and His Friend.*

1871   *Faust,* Part II. *Library of Travel.* Moved to New York; tried
       to sell or rent "Cedarcroft."

1872   *The Masque of the Gods; Beauty and the Beast & Tales of
       Home.* Death of Horace Greeley.

1873   *Lars: A Pastoral of Norway.*

1874   *The Prophet: A Tragedy; Egypt and Iceland in the year 1874;
       A School History of Germany.*

1875   *Home Pastorals, Ballads & Lyrics;* new, cheap edition of *Faust.*

1876   Returned to regular work at the *Tribune.* Read ode at cen-
       tennial celebration in Philadelphia. Lectured at Peabody
       Institute in Baltimore. *The Echo Club;* and *Boys of Other
       Countries.*

Chronology

1877 Lectured in New York, Brooklyn, Cornell, and Lowell Institute in Boston. Translated Schiller's *Don Carlos* for Lawrence Barrett.

1878 Appointed minister to Germany. Arrived there in May; suffered frequent illness as a result of exhaustion, diagnosed as a liver ailment. *Prince Deukalion.* Died December 19, 1878; body returned to Kennett Square; buried in Longwood Cemetery.

1879 *Studies in German Literature.*

1880 *Critical Essays and Literary Notes; The Dramatic Works of Bayard Taylor; The Poetical Works of Bayard Taylor.*

CHAPTER 1

Bayard Taylor
and the Genteel Tradition

BAYARD TAYLOR, who was born in Kennett Square, Pennsylvania, on January 11, 1825, was descended from farmers of English and German ancestry. They had been Quakers, and many family practices remained Quakerish in an area generally inhabited by Quakers. His early life was not remarkable; suffice it to say that he was uninterested in farming, was attracted to books and drawing, and early began writing verse of a feeble sort. When Taylor was twelve, his father was elected sheriff of the county; and the family moved to West Chester for three years, where Bayard attended Bolmar's academy. At fifteen, he published his first piece, an account of a visit to the Brandywine battlefield, in the West Chester *Register;* his first poem was printed in *The Saturday Evening Post* the following year.

His formal education ended at seventeen; he wanted to go to college, but the family could not afford to send him. Instead, he was apprenticed to a printer in West Chester for four years but served only one. Believing himself unsuited to such work, he followed the advice of Rufus Griswold and published his first volume of verse by subscription. With the money from this venture, plus commitments from various publishers for travel letters, he bought out the rest of his apprenticeship and traveled to Europe. The trip, beginning when he was nineteen and lasting over two years, was his Grand Tour and a substitute for a college education.

His biographer Albert Smyth has said that Taylor had a "delicately adjusted nervous organization" which "shrank from the coarse and homely duties of the garden and the field."[1] This

17

diagnosis may have been true; but it is also true that Taylor
was ultimately a big man; over six feet tall, he, in his maturity,
weighed over two hundred pounds. He was seldom ill; and,
if he had been delicate in childhood, one might not have guessed
it from his later years. According to Smyth, he was also full of
personal magnetism "to his finger tips."[2] Evidently, he was
handsome and personable, and attractive to many kinds of people.

When he returned from his European tour and published
Views A-Foot, he had his first taste of literary success. Besides
the encouraging sales of the book, he received congratulations
from Longfellow and Whittier; and he had his first reception
in Boston by the New England Worthies. He soon decided he
needed a steady income; he bought a newspaper in Phoenixville,
Pennsylvania; but, after a year of unsuccess, sold it and determined to make a literary career in New York. He went there in
December, 1847, to work for five dollars a week on Charles
Fenno Hoffman's *Literary World* and to teach school for four
dollars more.

It was Taylor's fate that, while the New York literary world
at this time was lively, with many authors, papers, and magazines
competing for place, not many were first-rate. The leading lights
were William Cullen Bryant, Fitz-Greene Halleck, and Nathaniel Willis. Washington Irving was in retirement at Tarrytown;
James Fenimore Cooper, who was living upstate, had not many
years left; nor had Edgar Allan Poe, who died in 1849. James
Kirke Paulding's career was nearly over, and Melville's had
hardly begun (but he, too, moved to New York in 1847). In
such a world (amusingly depicted in *John Godfrey's Fortunes*),
Taylor's talent seemed important; and, in short order, he
was receiving offers of all kinds. He was invited to edit *The
Union Magazine* and *Christian Inquirer* while its editor was in
Europe, to write book reviews for James Lorimer Graham, to become the New York correspondent of *The Saturday Evening Post,*
and to edit *Graham's Magazine.* "To no kind of newspaper duty
was he averse," said Smyth. "He wrote fifteen hours a day."[3] His
best offer, however, was from Horace Greeley; and in January,
1848, Taylor began a lifelong association with *The New York
Tribune.*

His first foreign assignment was a trip to California during
the gold rush which resulted in *Eldorado,* one of his best and

most popular travel books. When he returned to New York in March, 1850, his pay was increased; and he also became a shareholder in the *Tribune*. In August, 1851, he set out on a personal trip through the Middle East, which became ultimately a commissioned assignment for the *Tribune,* particularly when he accompanied Commodore Perry's expedition to Japan. Between this time and 1869, when he gave up traveling, he devoted a large portion of his time to wandering over the world; and he produced some ten volumes of travel narratives which fixed him in the minds of many as the "Great American Traveller," a title he hated. Of course, he also published during this same period ten other books of fiction and verse; but it was through the travel and subsequent lecture tours that Taylor became famous. Indeed, even many of his friends thought of him primarily as a traveler, though he worked hard to convince them otherwise. One of these was Whittier, who, in *The Tent on the Beach,* presented Taylor as

> One whose Arab face was tanned
>   By tropic sun and boreal frost,
> So traveled there was scarce a land
>   Or people left him to exhaust,
> In idling mood had from him hurled
>   The poor squeezed orange of the world,
> And in the tent-shade, as beneath a palm,
> Smoked, cross-legged like a Turk, in Oriental calm.[4]

In between travels and writing about them, Taylor worked feverishly, however, at two things: making money and creating a reputation as a poet. Unfortunately, the quest for money absorbed most of his time; he was constantly lecturing (though he hated that, too), writing articles, reviews, reports, verses, stories, novels. A great deal of this work was aimed at acquiring his splendid baronial mansion in Kennett Square, entertaining generously, and living luxuriously. But, despite all the money he made, he seemed constantly pressed for more; and, after the Civil War, when his popularity declined, his income was drastically reduced. He was finally driven in his last years to a desk in the *Tribune* office and to regular editorial work.

The careful cultivation of a poetic reputation was one of the most marked features of Taylor's career. He not only quickly found his way around in the New York literary jungle but also discovered how literary reputations were created. He became good friends with his publisher, James T. Fields, partly because they were men with similar tastes, partly because Fields's publishing house was most prestigious for poetry, but also partly because Fields knew how to sell books and create reputations. Taylor cultivated editors and publishers who might someday be useful; and, while he wrote many book reviews, he seldom said things that might create enemies. He was always careful to review his friends' books favorably, and he expected them to do the same for him. In other words, he was quite aware of the political means of creating a reputation, though, of course, he felt this maneuvering necessary to give good poetry its best start. He does not seem to have thought anything wrong with it; and, in his defense, it might be said that much the same conditions probably exist today. Literary success is still often determined to some extent by acquaintance with editors, publishers, agents, reviewers, and so on.

Taylor, whose first wife died shortly after their marriage, was married a second time, in 1857, to a German woman, Marie Hansen; they had a daughter in 1858. The marriage was partly a result of his strong German interests which had begun with his spending a year in Frankfurt during his first trip to Europe and which had been reinforced by his curious friendship with August Bufleb, whom he met on his Eastern trip. His interest in German literature and life grew steadily, as did his role of intermediary between German and American literature. This interest culminated in two important developments: his translation of *Faust* and his eventual appointment as the American minister to Berlin in 1878.

The nineteenth century was a great age for literary men in diplomacy, with John Hay, Washington Irving, Willard Motley, Nathaniel Hawthorne, William Dean Howells, and many others occupying such posts. Taylor, too, was interested in such a career partly as a result of his wide travel but more probably because of the steady income such a position provided. His first experience was with Commodore Perry's expedition to Japan; when he returned from that trip, he tried to secure the post as the first United States commissioner to Japan; but he was eventually disappointed. He did become attaché at St. Petersburg, Russia, in 1862; and, although he expected a ministership to follow, he was again disappointed. When he expected to become minister to Persia, that hope dwindled away in political confusion. In the mid-1870's, other appointments were rumored— to Brussels, for instance—but he held out for the one he wanted, Berlin, and finally attained it. The terrible irony is that he held this job, which he had wanted so badly, for only a short time: he arrived in Berlin in May, 1878, and died in December.

The last few years of his life, after giving up travel, Taylor spent on his poetry and more scholarly occupations. His work on *Faust* had developed the intellectual and critical turn of his mind, and he began giving lectures on German literature after he was named nonresident Professor of German at Cornell University. Part of his desire to be minister to Germany was that he planned a biography of Goethe and Schiller, which he unfortunately did not live to complete. Taylor had important qualities of a scholarly and critical nature that, in our day, might have made him an outstanding college professor.

But Taylor was essentially a journalist and a good one. Like many journalists, even today, he had literary aspirations. Since many American writers were journalists at some time during their careers—Ernest Hemingway, William Faulkner, Theodore Dreiser, H. L. Mencken—such a description of him is not denigration. If he did not have quite the talent, or genius, to achieve first-rate status in poetry, he made a noble attempt. The conditions under which he was forced to work made it very difficult, or nearly impossible, to attain what he wanted. He had, nonetheless, a good bit of talent; indeed, he was an intelligent man with great ability, but the world in which he operated hampered him greatly. The Genteel Tradition saddled him with a set of attitudes he was unable to overcome and thereby made it impossible for him to realize his full potential.

I   *The Genteel Tradition*

The traditional image of the poet (or of any serious writer) is that of the man in the garret who labors faithfully for his art. Indifferent to rewards or popular recognition, he is confident that his art will sometime be recognized as the great work it is; meanwhile, he lives hand to mouth, enjoys small pleasures, and hopes for the best. The idea that a poet ought to be prosperous and live a comfortable material life did not originate in our time, but we have done much to make it easily possible. Rather, the tendency seems to have begun in the nineteenth century with the changes in the reading audience from an aristocratic few to the democratic many; and it became fairly common in the Victorian age. Most Victorian poets lived reasonably well— Lord Tennyson, Robert Browning, and Matthew Arnold in England; Longfellow, James Russell Lowell, Bryant, Whittier, and others in America. To live like a gentleman was a cardinal principle of Victorian gentility; and during this period writers evidently felt that they, too, should live like prosperous members of bourgeois society. This desire is one sign of the Genteel Tradition in literature.

There have been many definitions of the Genteel Tradition, but few remark about the economic aspect of it. The values of the tradition were such as develop from comfortable living and from an accompanying isolation from ordinary life. For example, one feature of Taylor's novels, as well as of other Genteel novels, is the curious absence of sexual activity, or its concealment beneath a fog of idealistic abstraction. Women are divided into two types, "nice" women and the "bad" ones; and passion is attributed only to lower-class people who, having no education, may indulge themselves animalistically. The suggestion is that well-bred people do not speak of such passions, or think of them, or perhaps don't even indulge in them. At its simplest, such people do not use certain "vulgar" words and expressions *because* they are used by "vulgar" people. This division was invented by upper-class people to separate themselves from lower-class ones.

The word "genteel" comes from the same source as "gentle" in "gentleman."[5] It originates at the point at which the English aristocracy gives way to the rising commercial and industrial middle class. As this class rose, achieving money and power, it sought to acquire the graciousness, taste, and culture that it imagined the aristocracy to possess. In the imitation of these aristocratic qualities by the middle class (often accurately duplicating their form without their substance), the Genteel Tradition began. The old aristocracy lived in immense mansions surrounded by parks; they lived on income from land, did no work, and cultivated esthetic and artistic (more often athletic and sporting) tastes. The classic development varied little from an English lord to the Rockefeller family. One meaning of "genteel," then, is the imitation by rising people in society of the values, interests, and tastes of those above them in the economic scale.

George Santayana, who invented the term "genteel tradition,"[6] defined it as, in one sense, a discrepancy between the American mind and the American will—the intellectual life and the practical life, respectively. He symbolized this difference by comparing a reproduction of a colonial mansion with a skyscraper. The American will, he said, inhabits the skyscraper, the realm of practical life and the province of the male. The American intellect inhabits the colonial house—the cultural life, and the province of the female. Santayana meant that Americans were energetic and original in their solutions to life's material problems; but, when they dealt with literature and culture, they were inevitably oriented to European, chiefly English, models; and much truth resides in this concept. During much of the nineteenth century, the influence of England was very strong on American literature; for nearly all forms, ideas, and attitudes of our writers— even when they consciously *wanted* to be American—were drawn from English models; and they imitated nothing more than the style of living of English writers.

It is not irrelevant that Santayana chose buildings to make his point, for the symbolism of houses was very much a part of the Genteel Tradition. Houses are still one of the chief ways of expressing status; the wealthier one is, the larger the house he wants—though it is unreasonable to imagine anyone actually living in a house of fifty rooms. But the great ideal of English life was country living, with a large mansion amid much acreage; and this ideal came to be that of many English writers and, in imitation, of American ones. Many American writers did acquire large houses, surrounded by acres of trees and fields, to which they usually gave a rustic name. Many who had visited Tennyson at "Farringford" were impressed not only by the poet, but also by the comfort and gentility of his house; and so American writers also gave their houses such fancy, rustic names as "Elmwood" (Lowell), "Sunnyside" (Irving), "Cedarmere" (Bryant), "Ponkapog" (Aldrich), "Craigie House" (Longfellow),

"The Old Manse" (Emerson). Of course, some others were so
perverse as to live in cities; and others did not name their
houses. But, generally, authors' houses were fancy enough for
there to be even a book about them (in a series about the houses
of famous people) by Taylor's friend, R. H. Stoddard.[7]

II *Cedarcroft: A Symbol*

Bayard Taylor also built himself a house, an enormous mansion, near the town of Kennett Square, Pennsylvania, across the
road from the old homestead. He named it "Cedarcroft," and
it was set in the midst of two hundred acres of land which he
had worked many years to acquire. He supervised the building
of the house, and he poured out a steady stream of money to
create exactly the house he wanted. He noted every detail, and
some years later he even wrote a series of articles about it.[8] He
wanted his house to be "large and stately, simple in its forms,
without much ornament . . . expressive of strength and permanence," he said. "The old halls and manor houses of England are
the best models for such a structure. . . ." Among the things
such a house should have (oddly enough) was a tower, one
"large enough for use as well as ornament. . . ." Into this house
he moved with his entire family in the summer of 1860, not long
before the outbreak of the Civil War. He paid fifteen thousand
dollars for it, he said in February, 1860; but he had exceeded
his estimates by five thousand dollars; when he moved into the
house he was, therefore, in debt.[9]

Architecturally speaking, the house was nondescript. It was
massive (the walls were two feet thick); and, as he specified,
the building was stately, strong, and permanent. He lavished
much attention on details; he once wrote his fellow poet George
Boker about a black-walnut mantelpiece that he wanted made
from his own design: "I wish but a single panel as keystone,
and on it, instead of a T, the old coat of arms of the Taylor
family, which I will send when I reach New York. It is simple
—a lion rampant, holding a scallop-shell in his paws, and three
of the same shells on the shield."[10]

When Taylor's family moved into the mansion in 1860, he was
delighted; they gave a theatrical, a farce written by Taylor and
his friend Stoddard. Here, he entertained frequently and lav-

ishly. Boker, Stoddard, E. C. Stedman, Lowell, James T. Fields, even Emerson enjoyed his generous hospitality. He loved "Cedarcroft"; he worked hard on the garden and the lawns, planting trees of every type and description, planting vegetables and fruits, experimenting with Latakia tobacco and exotic melons. He enjoyed being a landowner, being the head of a large family, playing the generous and gracious host, and having the biggest house with the tallest tower in the surrounding country.

"Cedarcroft" was a fine symbol of Taylor himself—his tastes and desires, his dreams and hopes, his values, his success. It is also a symbol of the Genteel Tradition; its English antecedents are obvious—the country home, its size, and the kind of life lived there were essentially English. To Taylor, it also represented his success and wealth, and his admission into the company of Genteel authors who dominated American literature. He was all the more successful in that, when the house was completed in 1860, he was only thirty-five years old. But he was also the author of fourteen published volumes, he was known far and wide as a traveler and lecturer, and he was known (he hoped) among the cognoscenti as a poet of great promise.

But things began to go wrong with his house, as well as with his life. In the first place, he loved "Cedarcroft" all the more because he was seldom there; he was frequently traveling abroad. At first, he meant to live there all year; then he intended to spend his summers there and the winters in New York; but he spent only four of the first eight summers there. Not long after the house was finished, the Civil War began; and it changed everything for the worse. "Cedarcroft" was not far from the Maryland line, and for a while Taylor scurried around in panic, trying to find weapons and burying his books and manuscripts.

The invasion never materialized, but the house proved expensive to maintain, and the war affected his income. Lecture invitations diminished, sales of his books declined, his investment in the *Tribune* paid little. He was forced to work even harder—to write nearly anything to get money to pay his debts. He went to Europe to save money, living with his wife's family; in 1862 he became chargé d'affaires at St. Petersburg, but the job lasted only a year.

Finally, the joy and novelty of the house faded completely, and it became a burden, one increased by friction with the

neighbors. "He was driven by the demands which his estate
made upon him," said his wife; a "constant stream of ignominious
troubles was wearing away his patience, and gradually lessen-
ing the enthusiasm with which he had turned to Cedarcroft as
containing the satisfaction of his earthly desires."[11] In 1870,
only ten years after the joyous housewarming, Taylor burst out
to his mother that he was sick and tired of the place. It had
cost him five thousand dollars to maintain during his last European trip, and he had received no return from it. "Ever since
the house was built there have been but two years (1865 and
1866) when I was tolerably free from care. If I had known,
in 1859, how prices were to change, and labor to be dear and
unreliable, and the neighborhood to go backwards instead of
forwards, I never should have built at all," he said.[12] "It is
wrong," he added, "to waste the prime of life . . . or sacrifice it
to a sentiment." What he really wanted to do was live in New
York where "all the associations" were that he needed as an
author. "In short," he said, "my attempt to combine farming
and literature is a dead failure, and I have been carrying it on
now for several years . . . out of stubborn unwillingness to admit
that I was mistaken."[13]

He tried to sell the place, without success. He finally rented
it out while he was in Europe, but the tenant was untrustworthy
and gave Taylor no end of trouble. In the fall of 1874 he wrote
Stedman that he meant to keep "Cedarcroft" as a home for his
parents until there was a good chance of selling it. By 1875 he
had "given up" "Cedarcroft" to his sister and brother-in-law and
his parents. Though he still occasionally visited there, he now
made his home in New York City.

If one asks what the house meant to Bayard Taylor, it was
obviously the tangible symbol of his success. He had been a
poor farm boy, without notable antecedents, and without college education; but he liked writing and had discovered that
(in his world) writers who were successful lived well. He par-
layed some talent, a lot of luck and charm, and a propitious
time into a career of remarkable success, which he nurtured
with shrewdness. Seeing the money come in so easily, he took
it while he could; and he turned his hand to nearly every kind of
literary work to make the most of his name and fame. He

made the mistake, however, of thinking that it would always be that way.

Most literary men admire tradition, and Hawthorne was not the first American to bewail the country's lack of it. In "Cedarcroft" Taylor created for his family an estate that would become the traditional family acreage. It amounted to a sort of instant tradition—the quick creation of a baronial setting comparable to that of any of the New England Brahmins. But, in a way, the fact that he could afford such a house was concrete demonstration of the superiority of the American system. He did not emphasize this factor; indeed, he held views similar to British class distinctions, though his indifference to common people and peasants may have been just as German as English. Nonetheless, he always supported staunchly American democracy as he understood it—the right of the talented to rise above the mass. Such attitudes may help explain the resentment of his Kennett Square neighbors, though he found them utterly baffling.

But "Cedarcroft" was also a refuge for Taylor from the hectic, busy, and vulgar world; and he did much of his writing there. He collected a fine library, had a quiet study in the tower, had any number of servants and family to wait on him—as supporter of a large ménage, he deserved this attention. From here he would sally out into the world, travel over the globe, see Hottentots and Lapps, yet always have a center of warmth and hospitality to which to return. In this way he was able to produce some awful writing with perfect aplomb. Little in his experience urged him into new or original directions. He knew unconsciously that his continued comfort depended on producing more or less the same things, on pleasing the public who bought his books and attended his lectures—or, more accurately, on pleasing the editors who controlled what was published. In such ways was the Genteel Tradition perpetuated; it was profitable for those who were part of it.

Yet, to Taylor's credit, he reached a point of questioning doubt, symbolized by his doubts about the efficacy of owning a mansion. Why labor to write trivial pieces to support a level of living he did not need? He came to realize that he had used his substance to live as he had imagined literary men were supposed to. He began to see that success might be something else; that literary quality might be defined in other ways. Although he was never able to give up journalism completely, he dropped travel writing and lecturing; and he turned more and more to poetry and translating. He was living all the while more modestly—perforce, it is true; but he had also become less interested in the varieties of experience and more in its meaning. He became finally more scholarly, with his translation of *Faust* and with his research for the biographies of Goethe and Schiller. Perhaps his ultimate tragedy is that he came to see a better way, but by that time he was exhausted—or perhaps he simply lacked the imagination to achieve greater creative work.

CHAPTER 2

Travel Writings

"You ask, when will my wanderings end? God only knows. For me they are an absolute necessity; I owe my life and my success to them. . . ."—Letter to Boker, 1856.

"Bayard Taylor has travelled more and seen less than any man living."—Park Benjamin.

ON July 1, 1844, when the packet *Oxford* sailed from New York for Liverpool, Bayard Taylor, aged nineteen, was traveling second cabin with two friends—a cousin, Frank Taylor, and a neighbor, Barclay Pennock. For Taylor it was the beginning of a journey that lasted for the rest of his life; for traveling (not always willingly) was to become his fame and career. At the time, however, all he knew was that this trip was his Grand Tour. As Herman Melville's Ishmael said that a whale ship was his Yale and Harvard, so this trip was Taylor's university education. And Taylor, who had little more than good wishes from his family, had, in the best American tradition, earned the trip all by himself—and rather ingeniously.

First, though only nineteen, he was already a published author; in 1844, he had published a volume of his own poems by subscription. He then used the published book when visiting editors in New York and Philadelphia in seeking commissions. He sold some poems to James Lorimer Graham, and got commissions for travel letters from *The Saturday Evening Post, The United States Gazette,* and Horace Greeley. He had a total of one hundred and forty dollars; and since his passage cost only ten dollars (provisions and other expenses brought the total to twenty-four dollars), he was well on his way to fulfilling his dream of visiting Europe, and to a career.

But he could not travel luxuriously; his was to be a walking tour of the Continent. He did not mind, so powerful was his desire to travel; besides, he was healthy and vigorous, and had already some practice at long walks. He and his cousin had walked most of the way from Kennett Square, Pennsylvania, to and from Washington, D.C., to get a passport from their congressman. Indeed, it was probably the walking element that fascinated the public with his subsequent book; for, in two years, Taylor had walked over much of Europe. Moreover, the letters Taylor had sent to the various papers were well received and had prepared the ground for the book he published on his return in 1846. *Views A-Foot*, with an introduction by the champion introducer of the day, Nathaniel P. Willis, was immensely popular, going through six editions in the first year of publication and twenty editions by 1855.

Later in life, Taylor was puzzled and annoyed by the book's continued popularity: "Perhaps the want of development which the book betrays makes it attractive to those passing through the same phase of mental growth. I cannot otherwise account for its continued vitality."[1] His usual attitude was that his next book would be his best; besides, because he wanted to be known as a poet, the success of his travel books embarrassed him. Nonetheless, *Views A-Foot* laid the foundations of his career, and it should be carefully considered.

I   Views A-Foot (*1846*)[2]

The travel book as a literary genre has been insufficiently examined; and, though its popularity has slipped between Taylor's time and ours, its popular appeal is by no means dead. Then, however, the travel book constituted one chief source of a writer's income. Normally, a writer spent a year or so traveling, either to some place no one else had been or to a familiar place which he would try to "do up" in a different way. He would compile a book from his experiences, and probably some lectures to give on the circuit for a year or two. When the material was exhausted, he set off again in a new direction to get material for another book and more lectures. This method Taylor followed, and he managed to make his travel financially profitable three times: his material usually appeared first as letters in *The New*

York Tribune while he was on the move, then as books, and finally as lectures. He squeezed as much use from his travel material as it seems possible to extract. But travel writing was popular; and such books constituted, after all, a large portion of the work of Mark Twain; even Henry James produced several travel volumes.

Modern travel writing differs, however, from that of the past century because of the development of the photograph and of practical means of photo-printing. The older form placed a premium on descriptive writing; but, with the advent of the photograph, travel writers were forced to other emphases, such as mood, tone, and the "spirit of place." Scully Bradley identified good nineteenth-century travel books as seeking in some way to answer the question, "What shall I, as an American, do about Europe?"[3] This emphasis is interesting, but the travel book of a later age was less American-centered. The author is more interested in the quality of a place that separates it from any other. Of course, the difference between good and bad travel writing is often between the writer who takes the form seriously and the pedestrian one who simply wants to get his book on the market.

Many elements of the travel book made their way into fiction, and we have had many novels that give an account of life in other countries. Malcolm Lowry's *Under the Volcano,* F. Scott Fitzgerald's *Tender is the Night,* and James Baldwin's *Giovanni's Room*—these would make only the beginning of a long list. Even our idea of some countries comes from novelists—George Orwell's Burma, Andre Malraux's China, Hemingway's Spain, and Albert Camus's Algeria. It may be that the modern novelist is faced with the similar problem of a search for material after he has published a couple of books.

One of the peculiar things about some nineteenth-century fiction writers was their failure to make much use of their travel experience in fiction. For example, Mark Twain seldom used foreign settings for his fiction, except for a medieval world he drew from reading. Similarly, Bayard Taylor became a highly sophisticated world traveler; yet in his four novels little trace of this experience can be found. They are nearly all local-color stories; and we are confronted with a body of fiction which deals almost entirely with Kennett Square, Pennsylvania.

But the earlier nineteenth-century travel book—according to Bradley, that of the "less imaginative of the professional writers" —followed a standard pattern:

The author must begin with the excitements of the ocean voyage itself and devote at least a portion of a chapter to the thrill, so long anticipated, of setting foot on foreign soil. From this point on he should mix architecture and scenery with comment on philanthropies, skillfully work in a little history cribbed from Murray's guides, taking care to add a touch of sentiment or eloquence when the occasion permitted. If the essay or book required a little padding, it was always possible to retell an old legend or slip in an account of dangers surmounted in crossing the Alps.[4]

While deviations from this pattern developed later, as Bradley has noted, the reader of the 1850's and 1860's wanted a series of variations on a theme: "It did not matter to him that he had read forty descriptions of the hallowed places—Shakespeare's tomb, the Burns country, Warwick Castle, and the Tower of London, the Vale of Chamonis, and the Roman Campagna. He listened with delight to any new variations. . . ."[5] With this pattern in mind, one should more closely view Taylor's first travel book, *Views A-Foot.*

Taylor left the ship at Liverpool and toured Ireland and Scotland first. He marveled at the Giant's Causeway, but did not care much for the Irish: "On many of their countenances there was scarcely a mark of intelligence." On the other hand, he liked Scotland; he climbed Ben Lomond, visited Glasgow, and attended the Robert Burns festival. He was shocked to find Burns's cottage a tavern, and hastened away: "there was profanity in the thought." (He quickly lost, however, his youthful temperance attitudes.) At Sir Walter Scott's Abbotsford he felt "an awe in treading these lonely halls like that which impressed me before the grave of Washington." He walked from Edinburgh over the English border; and, seeing a group of locked-out miners in Newcastle who were singing for charity, his blood boiled—"to hear those tones wrung from the heart of Poverty by the hand of Tyranny." In London, he saw the sights for a week. Westminster Abbey thrilled him: "What a glorious galaxy of genius is here collected! What a constellation of stars whose light is immortal! The mind is completely fettered by their spirit." He especially liked paintings of the Virgin and child, and he found a Murillo in the National Gallery that had "an innocence, a childish sweetness of expression, in the countenance, which makes one love to gaze on it." But all was not rosy; there was much crime in London: and "one sees enough of degradation and brutality in a short time to make his heart sick."

He stayed in Germany for a full year, making frequent trips by foot from Frankfurt. Much of his writing is description of scenery; he visited castles and museums, commented on art and architecture, recited local legends and stories, and included some of his own poems. Considering his mode of travel, he didn't comment much on the life of ordinary Germans, though he remarked about inns, food, or people he met. He visited Heidelberg several times, once going to a student beer hall, later watching a duel. He was ecstatic over Beethoven's opera *Fidelio*—"one of the most perfectly beautiful creations that ever emanated from the soul of genius .... My nerves were thrilled till I could bear no more. . . ."

He was never idle during a long, cold winter in Frankfurt. He visited a school for the deaf and also visited Mendelssohn; he walked to Cassell, to the Hartz Mountains, to the Brocken. In May, he visited Leipzig and Dresden, where he found another Madonna and Child, this one by Raphael, which "had so grown into my love and admiration that it was painful to think I should never see it again." In Vienna, he attended a concert by Johann Strauss and visited the graves of Beethoven and Schubert. In a Viennese museum, he managed to find another child painting, Correggio's Cupid, "a picture which 'stings the brain with beauty.' " He visited Freiburg and the Black Forest, and he met the poet Freiligrath—the greatest German poet of the day, he said, next to Uhland.

As for Italy, Taylor did not think much of it; the people were "coarse, ignorant and savage-looking, the villages remarkable for nothing except the contrast between splendid churches and miserable, dirty houses." The Italians, he said, "are indolent and effeminate. Of the moral dignity of man they have little conception .... The state of morals is lower than in any other country of Europe; what little virtue exists is found among the peasants . . . ." He especially disliked priests, who were everywhere; and he fancied he could see in their faces "the traces of passions that burned within." But he liked Italian art and architecture, though disappointed in a performance of *Wilhelm Tell*. Taylor's mode of dining in Italy was interesting: "At the common inns where we stopped we always met with civil treatment, though, indeed, as we only slept in them, there was little chance of practising imposition. We bought our simple meals at the baker's and grocer's and ate them in the shade of the grape-bowers, whose rich clusters added to the repast" (281).

After Genoa, Livorno, and Pisa came Florence. As usual, he visited the galleries, but was offended by Michelangelo's "Drunken Bacchus," thinking the artist's talents might "have been employed better than in ennobling intoxication." About Fiesole, he wrote one of many "set pieces"—one also fairly typical of his descriptive prose: "Stand with me a moment on the height, and let us gaze on this grand panorama, around which the Apennines stretch with a majestic sweep, wrapped in a robe of purple air, through which shimmer the villas and villages on their sides . . ." (300). Unbelievably, he found another Madonna and Child, by Raphael, and he experienced a by-now predictable reaction: "I feel an impulse I can scarcely explain—a longing to tear it from the canvas as if it were a breathing form and clasp it to my heart in a glow of passionate love" (304).

Back in Florence, he visited frequently with American artists, the greatest of whom he thought was Hiram Powers, the sculptor of the "Greek Slave" and "Eve." With regret he left Florence for Rome, where his comments were devoted to the usual monuments, paintings, and buildings. Naturally, he visited the graves of Keats and Shelley; but, unable to visit Greece, he left Rome for Marseilles in mid-January. However, Taylor did not say much about France. He liked Marseilles for its cleanliness, but was not impressed by the countryside on the way to Vaucluse. By this time, he was living on virtually nothing, waiting for money to arrive from somewhere; and, by the time it did, he was anxious to get home. Though he spent five weeks in Paris, he devoted only one chapter to the usual sights; and, after seeing Versailles, he took a boat in March for England, where he remained until late April. In England, Taylor tried to get work as a printer; but without English papers that was impossible, though he did find some work with Putnam, the publisher. However, he said little about his English sojourn in this book. In late April, he was on a ship home, arriving in New York on June 1, 1846, after an absence of two years.

In the eighth edition of his *Views A-Foot* Taylor added the chapter "Advice and Information for Pedestrians," one of the most interesting things in the book; it gave in concrete detail how he lived, how much things cost, and what the entire trip had cost him—four hundred and seventy-two dollars and ten cents. This chapter is reminiscent of Thoreau because of its emphasis on cheapness and simplicity, and some of Taylor's advice is probably still good for those about to embark on walking tours.

Views A-Foot was not far from the typical nineteenth-century travel book described by Bradley. It mixes "architecture and scenery with comment on philanthropy"; it works in "a little history cribbed from Murray's guides"; there are many touches of sentiment and eloquence; and a number of old legends are retold. But Taylor's youth, if nothing else, could explain why he followed the pattern of earlier books—though it may not excuse his lack of originality. Yet, the book was immensely popular.

Views A-Foot was more than an average travel book; it was the quintessence of the average. Not only did it possess the qualities mentioned; it also embodied most of the "correct" attitudes of the time. For example, there is a pervasive patriotism running through it which undoubtedly pleased its American readers. Taylor frequently alluded to the superiority of American institutions, customs, and people. "How we had thought of the life, the neatness, the comfort, of our American cities, when rambling through some filthy and depopulated capital of the Old World!" is a fairly typical remark. He was proud to have "come from a new world, where the spirit of man is untrammelled by the mouldering shackles of the past" (77). Even American women were better looking: "I have seen more beautiful women in one night in a public assembly in America than during the seven months I have been on the continent" (121).

Despite his strong opinions about America, Taylor is, however, curiously class conscious. He was always aware of the social status of people he met, and he was frequently annoyed that his lack of money forced him to live mainly with the lower class. He considered himself an intellectual and a literary man who deserved better. His remarks about the lower classes were nearly always unfavorable: they drank a lot; and they were crude, vulgar, and animalistic. This set of attitudes seems an odd one for a "democratic" American to possess.

A second factor is that Taylor's tastes and attitudes about art were almost totally conventional. In paintings, he leaned heavily to "scenes," panoramic views, and idealized virgins and children —he also liked real children and young men, whom he often described in sculpturesque terms. His attitude toward art in general, including poetry, was that it was sacred, hallowed. "We are pilgrims to the shrines of Art and Genius," he said; "the dwelling-places of great minds are our sanctuaries" (307). He approached any work of art with piety; in the following passage, the art emotion merges with the religious:

Difficulty and toil give the soul strength to crush in a loftier region the passions which draw strength only from the earth. So long as we listen to the purer promptings within us there is a Power invisible, though not unfelt, who protects us; amid the toil and tumult and soiling struggle there is ever an eye that watches, ever a heart that overflows with infinite and almighty love. Let us trust, then, that eternal Spirit who pours out on us his warm and boundless blessings through the channels of so many kindred hearts. (343-44)

A third important factor in the success of the book was that Taylor had the right biases, ones shared by a great number of Americans. He is strongly anti-Roman Catholic, for example; he disliked the Church itself, its priests and monks, its "idolatry," and the way in which it "bamboozled" its followers. The condemnation of the Roman Church as a tyranny was a typical American attitude; even Hawthorne's views were similar, though more complex; and Mark Twain's, though later, were very close. Taylor was also anti-Semitic, not virulently, but in a genteel way. He thought he knew a Jew by sight: "There is something . . . about a Jew, whether English or German, which marks him from all others . . . . It lays [sic] principally in their high cheekbones, prominent nose and thin, compressed lips, which especially, in elderly men, gives [sic] a peculiar miserly expression . . ." (121). Similarly, his distate for Irish and Italians was probably "normal" for the time. Of course, Taylor did not omit the classic American criticism of foreign countries, one voiced even in our day—the dirtiness of both people and places; but Taylor did not emphasize it so much as Twain did.

One cannot help feeling that a fourth popular quality of the book was the sheer superficiality of its observations. Taylor never penetrated very far into anything; he merely described externals. He might reply, of course, that that was all he tried to do; one cannot go deeper unless he stays in one place. Yet he stayed in Germany a full year, and his observations there were not significantly better than elsewhere. On some occasions he did remark on social problems or disturbing government practices, but his comment was usually a conventional disapproval. In the passage quoted earlier about English miners on strike, he can only lapse into abstraction—the Hand of Tyranny squeezing Poverty—and its implication is largely patriotic: such things don't happen in America. Generally speaking, *Views A-Foot* is pedestrian in more senses than one.

But the "A-Foot" part of the book gave it novelty. His observations may not be original; the places he visited may have been the usual ones; he may have seen things only through a conventional haze; but the spectacle of a young American who left for Europe with such supreme confidence and without much money showed the superiority of the American fiber. In its way, Taylor's is a version of the success story; and this quality may have been one chief reason for the book's popularity.

Of course, the book is that of an impressionable and a very young man. In later life, Taylor freed himself from many of the attitudes expressed in it, and developed others more sensible. No doubt some of the faults of the book are traceable to a lack of education, although Taylor's self-education eventually became quite extensive. Yet the book is curiously impersonal. Taylor reveals little of himself; or, perhaps because he was so young and naive, there was as yet little to reveal.

II   Eldorado (1850)[6]

In the late 1840's the discovery of gold in California caused great excitement in the East. Although the recent war with Mexico had made people conscious of the Far West, knowledge of the area was very hazy, and communication with it was very slow. Suddenly California and gold were big news, and it was

appropriate that Horace Greeley chose Bayard Taylor to report
the gold rush since he was already an experienced traveler.
Taylor was already interested in California; he had published
several poems in the *Literary World* which he called "Californian" ballads. They were purely imaginative, but they show that
the area existed in his mind as an exotic, primitive place. He had
already thought about going there; and, when the chance came
to go at the *Tribune's* expense, he was delighted.

The book he made from this trip sealed his fate as a travel
writer. *Views A-Foot* had laid the groundwork, but *Eldorado*
set his other foot, as it were, firmly in the path of travel writing,
no matter what he may have said he wanted to do. Travel was
to become too profitable for him to give up; besides, he liked it,
especially in the early years. One observer said of him that he
was "a wanderer, to the very heart and core of his being . . .
who . . . yearned always for the lands beyond this world's narrow
rim."[7] This judgment is a reasonably accurate one.

So Taylor sailed from New York on June 28, 1849, eight
months after the news reached the East, to Cuba, to New Or-
leans, to Chagres in Panama. He crossed the Isthmus by canoe
and horseback in five days of "roughing it." Then from Panama
City, he went up the West Coast to San Francisco, arriving
fifty-one days after he had left New York. His account of this
journey is interesting, accurate, and even amusing. Some of his
meals consisted of "pieces of pork fat, with fresh bread and a
draught of sweet spring water," which he found delicious. His
first experience of tropical foliage taxed his descriptive powers:
"No description that I have ever read conveys an idea of the
splendid overplus of vegetable life within the tropics . . . . All
the gorgeous growths of an eternal summer are so mingled in
one impenetrable mass that the eye is bewildered" (13). Sometimes his optimism, too, was strained; for he had a low opinion
of some people he saw, such as a "choice gang of blacklegs . . .
going out to extend the area of their infernal profession."

But San Francisco, he said, was hard to believe: "One knows
not whether he is awake or in some wonderful dream. Never
have I had so much difficulty in establishing, satisfactorily to
my own senses, the reality of what I saw and heard" (44). It
was a marvelous mixture of peoples, and a feverish activity
with money in vast sums. Even the streets were constantly

gleaned by children, who made a few dollars a day. Prices were absurd: a ten-by-twenty-five foot tent rented for forty thousand dollars a year, while the Parker House rented for one hundred and ten thousand.

When Taylor went on a trip by muleback to the San Joaquin Valley, he met and was impressed by Colonel John C. Frémont. He watched the miners on the Mokelumne, and he concluded that "those who pave streets and quarry limestone are best adapted for gold-diggers." With his preconceptions, Taylor couldn't admit that gold digging was a matter of luck. He scorned sore losers, and he argued that "there is no such thing as accident in Nature, and in proportion as men understand her, the more sure a clue they have to her buried treasures" (69). His views of law and order were equally sanguine: "there was as much order and security as could be attained without a civil organization." Punishments were severe—whipping, cropping, hanging; he witnessed the whipping of some Negroes and was disturbed by onlookers who "jeered, laughed, and accompanied every blow with coarse and unfeeling remarks." He was confident that, as emigration increased, law would become "more orderly and intelligent." Hospitality existed in those rude tents, nonetheless, proving that "abundance of gold does not always beget, as moralists tell us, a grasping and avaricious spirit" (79).

He decided to walk to Monterey to report upon the state constitutional convention. On the way, he commented on ranches, crops, and climate; and he prophesied that "the vine will hereafter be an important product of California, and even Burgundy and Tokay may be superseded on the tables of the luxurious by the vintage of San Jose and Los Angeles" (96). Monterey he found to be more dignified than San Francisco; indeed, it had the best society outside of Los Angeles. There were "racial" problems, however, since native Californians (Spanish-descended persons) were quickly outnumbered by emigrants from the East; yet the Easterners were a factor tending to law and order. The convention did a good job, however, and he said: "As an American, I feel proud and happy—proud that the Empire of the West, the commerce of the great Pacific, the new highway to the Indies, forming the last link in that belt of civilized enterprise which now clasps the world, has been established under my country's flag; and happy that in all the extent of California . . .

no slave shall ever lift his arm to make the freedom of that flag a mockery" (125).

When Taylor soon felt "the old impatience and longing for motion and change," he returned to San Francisco. He visited Sacramento City, then rode horseback through the mountains, winding up again on the Mokelumne to observe the miners on election day. He enjoyed their company: "It was never safe to presume on a person's character from his dress or appearance. A rough, dirty, sunburned fellow, with unshorn beard, quarrying away for life at the bottom of some rocky hole, might be a graduate of one of the first colleges in the country, and a man of genuine refinement and taste" (192). The miners also indulged themselves; in the middle of nowhere, Taylor was served such things as smoked tongue, oysters, and fresh butter.

But, since the rainy season was beginning, he returned to San Francisco, where he concluded that, in spite of all the "dissipating and disorganizing influences, the main stock of society was sound, vigorous, and progressive." When he left on January 1, 1850, he was convinced that "California should be the most democratic country in the world" (236).

On his return trip to the East, Taylor decided to visit Mexico; and, after sailing south of Mazatlan, he journeyed by foot and muleback to Vera Cruz, a distance of twelve hundred miles. The trip, some said, was foolhardy, but he was unafraid; and the result was one of the few accounts of the area at that time. He scorned stories of Mexican cheating: "During all my travels in the Tierra Caliente, I was never imposed upon as a stranger nor insulted as an American" (256). Mexicans "acknowledged our greater power and intelligence as a nation," he said; however, he was robbed by bandits near Guadalajara, but he suffered no physical harm.

Of Mexican art, he said that many cathedrals "are spacious and might be made impressive, but they are all disfigured by a tawdry and tasteless style of ornament, a profusion of glaring paint and gilding, ghastly statues, and shocking pictures" (284). He stayed in Mexico City a week, visiting battlefields of the war. He finally reached Vera Cruz, took an English ship on February 19, and arrived in New York on March 10 after a trip of eight months and eight days.

He had been negotiating with Putnam for his proposed book

even before he left California; and he felt sure of "doing some-thing with it which may be of lasting credit."[8] Putnam did publish *Eldorado* in 1850; it also appeared in England, and a German translation appeared the next year. Very popular, it went through ten editions in thirty years. It also has the distinc-tion of being Taylor's most recently reprinted travel book, for the California Centennial of 1949 was marked by a new edition from Knopf, with Taylor's own illustrations, tinted. (It should be mentioned that his drawings were not bad; he had a lifetime interest in sketching and painting, though his drawings were not always included in his books.)

Eldorado is also one of his best travel books: it is lively, full of detail, cheerful, and vigorous. He shows more command of his prose, and also more confidence in his judgments. It is also more unified, and it is more interesting because the places he visited were new. It is also less literary, for he had fewer oppor-tunities to genuflect to art, architecture, and other forms of beauty. Moreover, this book is historically important since it was one of the earliest accounts of the gold fields. Of course, there is still too much of the "picturesque" in it; but his observa-tion is often sharp, perceptive, and interesting. Of all Taylor's talents, he was a first-class journalist; and his *Tribune* train-ing had given him the experience he needed to create an effective book.

Beatty, who complained of Taylor's optimism in this book, suggested that Taylor was ordered by Greeley to produce a cheerful account.[9] But all Taylor's books are optimistic and cheerful, especially the early ones. "I am going to tell the truth," he told his fiancée; "and I think I shall have a cheerful story to send home."[10] Taylor was not dishonest; he simply tended to see the good side. In fact, he reported many gloomy things—miners who had failed, whippings, men dying by the road with no one offering help; but they did not affect his total outlook, which emphasized the beauty of the country, its wealth, and its agricultural possibilities. In *Views A-Foot* he insisted that there was more good in people than most would concede; and in *Eldorado* he emphasized the natural tendency to law and order, and the hospitality and generosity of the people. His view was simply a matter of temperament, and Taylor's—at least at this time—was optimistic and cheerful.

III   A Journey to Central Africa (*1854*)[11]

Taylor's next trip, his longest and most extensive, was his famous journey through the African continent and the East which associated him in the public mind with the peoples of Africa and with the Arabs. He extracted three books from this trip, so it proved quite profitable not only in book sales but also in the demand for his lectures. (Another result was *Poems of the Orient,* his best-selling book of verse.) He did so well, in fact, that he was able to begin acquiring the land for "Cedarcroft." This trip was not originally commissioned; he was naturally drawn to the mystery of the Orient, and he also needed to get away from editorial drudgery.

But Taylor also had a personal reason; since his return from California, Taylor's fiancée, Mary Agnew, had become incurably ill. Taylor had delayed marrying her until he was more firmly established financially; but now they were hurriedly married on October 24, 1850. ("She wished to bear my name for a few days, at least," he wrote Fields); and she died two months later. Taylor, suffering genuinely, "rolled a stone across the irrecoverable and unforgettable past"; and, as soon as he could, he left for Egypt. To finance the trip, he, in conjunction with George Ripley, edited for Putnam a *Cyclopaedia of Literature and the Fine Arts;* and Taylor confided to his friend Boker that "it's really not worth many words: a piece of hack-work I am doing for Putnam."[12] Yet, after the trip began, he wrote letters for the *Tribune,* so he was not without support; moreover, half of the trip was specifically commissioned by the *Tribune.*

The three books Taylor produced from this trip constitute a trilogy of Africa and the East, for they have a similarity of form, attitude, and temper. The first book was the most famous and is still the best: *A Journey to Central Africa.* He covered some territory on this trip that was comparatively new; few travelers in Egypt went as far as Khartoum, and few white men had ever gone beyond. Taylor, however, penetrated two hundred and fifty miles beyond to the land of the Shilook Negroes—farther, he said, than any American or Englishman had gone. In fact, he found it necessary to deny that he was looking for the source of the White Nile.

An important event on this trip was his meeting with August

Bufleb, a German businessman from Saxe-Coburg-Gotha, who became so enamored of Taylor that it is embarrassing. Bufleb wrote his wife, for example, that Taylor was "a glorious young man; if it were not for you I would go with him. He has won my love by his amiability, his excellent heart, his pure spirit, in a degree of which I did not believe myself capable."[13] Taylor, who reciprocated, wrote his mother that "when we speak of parting in a few days it brings the tears into our eyes";[14] but part they did, for Bufleb was unable to go to Khartoum. This friendship shows Taylor's remarkable ability to attract people, especially men, and the depth of such feelings. Bufleb proved a very important friend, for Taylor's later visits to Bufleb in Germany helped strengthen his interest in things German and also introduced him to Marie Hansen, who became his second wife in 1857.

Another important result of the trip was Taylor's taste for things Arabian. He was imaginatively drawn to the color and sensuousness of the Middle East, and it is no surprise that he found it largely as he had imagined. He displayed a genuine liking for the desert, for horses, for dancing girls, and for smoking the tarboosh. He enjoyed being treated like a visiting pasha; and, most of all, he loved the sensuousness of the bath, an institution he described in loving detail.

The book opens with an apology for haste of composition— a disclaimer found in nearly all of his travel books. He tried to give "correct pictures," he said, "a faithful narrative of my own experience," and "resisted the temptation to yield myself up to . . . more subtle and poetic aspects" (2). This remark seems to say that literal truth is preferable to imaginative—an odd attitude for a Romantic poet. Long stretches of this book are dull, for Taylor seems to feel that he must describe everything —hence the great detail about the landscape, population, agriculture, even commerce and taxes. Endless pages describe temples and monuments until the reader is surfeited; but Taylor was never surfeited visiting such places. In barren country, he concentrated on food or the appearance and habits of his companions.

Cairo was his favorite city, "the illuminated frontispiece to the volume of my Eastern life." The pyramids he approached "without the violent emotion which sentimental travelers experience, but with a quiet feeling of the most perfect satisfaction"

(58). With the help of three Arabs, he climbed the pyramid of Cheops in ten minutes, came down in six or seven, and promptly fainted. He visited the Sphinx and the ruins of Memphis, the graves of Beni-Hassan and tombs of Lycopolis. Much of his information is probably derived from guidebooks; for he hinted that he had prepared himself by reading standard works, so he was able to discourse learnedly, even on such topics as phallic worship.

As a traveler, Taylor left little to chance. He usually carried letters to officials who furnished comfortable quarters or smoothed the way for him. Even in the heart of Africa, he usually sought out the head man or pasha in each town or village; accepting their hospitality seemed to be his idea of living with the natives. But drifting down the Nile with Bufleb was the best life he could imagine: "I never before experienced such a thorough deliverance from all the petty annoyances of travel in other lands, such perfect contentment of spirit, such entire abandonment to the best influences of nature. Everyday opens with a *jubilate*, and closes with a thanksgiving" (86).

At Aswan, after Taylor and Bufleb had parted tearfully, Taylor went on to the Nubian desert, and hired camels for a trip across. "I found dromedary-riding not at all difficult," he said; "I rode from eight to ten hours a day, read and even dreamed in the saddle, and was at night as fresh and unwearied as when I mounted in the morning" (174). He liked the desert: "I found an unspeakable fascination in the sublime solitude of the Desert. I often beheld the sun rise, when, within the wide ring of the horizon, there was no other living creature to be seen. He came up like a god, in awful glory, and it would have been a natural act, had I cast myself upon the sand and worshipped him. . . . The scenery, so far from depressing, inspired and exhilarated me . . ." (182).

When Taylor reached Khartoum on January 12, 1852, he stayed with the Austrian consular agent and made excursions into the country by horseback. Khartoum society was various: "On the same day, I have had a whole sheep set before me, in the house of an Ethiopian Princess, who wore a ring in her nose; taken coffee and sherbet with the Pasha; and drank tea, prepared in the true English style, in the parlor of a European" (275). He decided, however, to go farther; he rented a boat and sailed up the White Nile to the island of Aba, two hundred and fifty miles beyond Khartoum, where crocodiles and other exotic life abounded. "This was Central Africa as I had dreamed it—a grand though savage picture, full of life and heat, and with a barbaric splendor even in the forms of Nature" (328).

Back in Khartoum, Taylor continued his round of visits and dinners, which he lovingly detailed. He praised the missionaries, "self-sacrificing" men willingly devoting themselves to an unpleasant life "for the sake of introducing a purer religion among its pagan inhabitants" (380). He arrived back in Cairo on April 1, 1852, staying only eight days. "I left Cairo with regret," he said, "as I left Thebes and the White Nile, and every other place which gives one all that he came to seek" (522).

II   Lands of the Saracen (*1854*)[15]

The second volume of the trilogy, *Lands of the Saracen,* was published four months after *Central Africa.* From Cairo, Taylor went to Alexandria, then to Beyrouth, where this volume begins April 14, 1852. He described his itinerary in a letter to Fields:

After seeing all Palestine and Syria, I coasted northwards from Beyrout [*sic*] to the mouth of the Orontes, and then traveled inland to Antioch and Aleppo. In Aleppo I stayed several days. It is a great and stately city, and pleased me even better than Damascus. I saw a great deal of society there, and attended both Christian and Hebrew weddings, balls, and other festivities. Thence I crossed the mountains into Cilicia, and after visiting ancient Tarsus, and drinking a cup of snow-cold water from the Cydnus at the very spot where Cleopatra met Mark Antony, struck northward into Asia Minor. I was three days passing the Taurus, by a defile grander than any in the Alps, and reached the plains of Karamania. Thence to Konieh, (the ancient Iconium), and so on into the glorious piny mountains of Phrygia, where I found the tombs of King Midas and the Gordian monarchs. Thence to Kiutahya, to the old Greek city of Oezani, with a magnificent theatre and temple, and over Olympus, through the sublimest beechen forests in the world, and down on the other side to Brousa. A voyage in an open boat across the Sea of Marmora finished the journey, and brought me here in time to see, last night, the superb illumination of the mosques and the Golden Horn, on the occasion of the Sultan's taking a new wife....[16]

This good bit of traveling still does not include all that he did. He also went to Smyrna, Malta, and Sicily, and saw an eruption of Mt. Aetna. On November 6 he was in Gibraltar, where he began a three-week journey through parts of Spain, returning to Gibraltar in late November.

Lands of the Saracen is rather dull; it bears many signs of hasty composition; and, since it is in diary form, it seems as if he didn't bother revising his journals. The book is very loose and contains several essayistic digressions, one of which describes his visions under hasheesh. These are curious, though not so interesting as those of DeQuincey, from whom Taylor probably borrowed the idea. The experience taught him "the majesty of human reason and human will" and "the awful peril of tampering" with such things. Other essays, on bathing, on pipes and coffee, are not bad examples of their genre. The one about bathing elicits the daring opinion that dress "hides from us much of the beauty and dignity of Humanity." Indeed, Taylor liked the naturalness and physicality of the East; and he thought Westerners should "preserve that healthy physical development . . . now only to be found among our semi-barbaric brethren" (311). The places visited have something to do with the dullness, for Taylor admitted that the book described "beaten tracks of travel" and that all his observations could claim was "sincerity" and "correct pictures." Of course, nineteenth-century travelers had to visit the Holy Land, and this is Taylor's Holy Land book. But he doesn't seem very much interested; after drifting down the Nile and crossing the desert by camel, this sort of travel seemed tame.

Taylor liked Moslems; the filthiest people in Jerusalem, he said, were Christians and Jews: "Were I cast here, ignorant of any religion, and were I to compare the lives and practices of the different sects as the means of making my choice . . . I should at once turn Musselman" (79). The same was true of Spain, where "one's sympathies are wholly with the Moors. The few mutilated traces which still remain of their power, taste, and refinement, surpass any of the monuments erected by the race which conquered them" (425). Modern Spaniards were "enslaved, ignorant and degenerate." On the other hand, he found the Turks repulsive; and he concluded that "the life of the Orient is nerveless and effete"; attempts to adopt Western institutions produced "mere galvanic spasms." He exhibited skepticism at the shrines of the Holy Land, but he remained strong in his conviction that Christianity was the best religion.

Taylor, who sometimes wore the costume of the country and used ordinary travel routes, wrote a friend that he was "determined to taste the Orient as it was, in reality, not as a mere outside looker-on." While such attempts were not always successful, it was perhaps most successful in Spain. Although he was not there very long, he at least didn't spend the time with the American ambassador; he traveled horseback and learned something of common life.

Lands of the Saracen is more relaxed than the earlier books; he has gained confidence and can even afford occasional, if strained, humor. Generally, his prose is at least competent; and the puzzle is why the prose of a poet is sometimes so dull. When his friend Stoddard complained that Taylor's prose books lacked "poetic and imaginative description," Taylor replied that his plan was to "keep poetry in one dish and prose in another, and let those mix them who choose."[17] Despite this odd rejoinder, Taylor actually slighted his prose because he didn't respect it enough; he wanted to be a poet, and most of his prose books were hastily written. He never tried very hard to work out anything in the travel-book form, despite the fact that such books were his bread and butter; they reveal him too often as hasty and careless but also as straightforward and intelligent. His prose gradually improved, however, and it is unfortunate that he hampered himself by an unrealistic ambition; if he had concentrated on prose, he might have developed into a stylist of some skill.

One reason for the popularity of these travel books was that they were quite long and offered a lot for the money—wads of information and facts, elaborate description, and (in some) his own illustrations. But the books also have a tone of easy assurance and knowledgeableness about art, occasional foreign words and phrases, references to literature, quotes from popular authors. All of these characteristics no doubt helped convey the impression to naive readers that they were acquiring culture. Taylor's attitude, too, is always cheerful, healthy, curious, and normal; he is adaptable, interested in people (though not profoundly), often hobnobs with the wealthy and famous. There is little speculation or profound criticism; he stays pretty much

with surfaces. Writing for a culture-hungry audience, he supplies its need; probably he was like his audience in many respects.

In a sense, too, these books flatter the American reader; for
they imply that, while the rest of the world may be older, larger,
and more various, there are few ways in which it excels America.
American institutions are superior; the climate, scenery, people,
traditions, and religion are all preferable. There are no smoky
opium dens, no unusual sexual practices, no barbaric food like
snails or ants, no sleepy bureaucracy battening off the people;
in short, there is no place like home.

V   India, China, and Japan   (1855)[18]

In Constantinople, Taylor heard from the *Tribune,* suggesting
that he accompany Commodore Perry's expedition to Japan. He
had been away nearly a year and was tired; but, on the other
hand, the *Tribune* offered him expenses and a higher rate for his
letters. Besides, Japan was still mysterious; and Taylor would
be one of the first Americans to see it. He wrote his mother:
"I am a little ambitious and the expedition offers chances which
I can't let slip of doing something which may make me honor. . . .
My magnetism urges me on, and when I follow it I always go
right. . . . I feel that it only needs for me to continue in the same
course I have begun to assure me fame and fortune."[19]

However, Commodore Perry first refused to permit Taylor to
accompany him; when pressure was brought to bear, he finally
arranged to meet Taylor at Hong Kong. So Taylor left Gibraltar
in November, 1852; touched at Alexandria, Cairo, Suez; sailed
down the Red Sea; crossed the Arabian Sea; and landed at
Bombay in December. He crossed India, usually by banghy-cart,
stopping at many cities to write descriptions of tombs and monuments. He reached Calcutta in February, went to Singapore, and
arrived in Hong Kong in March. Finally, in May, Perry's ship
appeared; Taylor met him and was appointed a master's mate
in the United States Navy. The reason for this appointment was
not far to seek: he was to be under Perry's immediate command.
"The rules of the service forbid me writing a line for publication and oblige me at the end of the cruise to give up my journal
to the Navy Department."[20] Every line he wrote for the *Tribune*
was censored; and, despite valiant efforts later, he never got
back his journal from the Navy Department.

Perry's ship sailed in May, 1853, to the Loo-Choo Islands (now the Ryukyus), the chief port of which was Napa (now Naha on the island of Okinawa); it also visited the Bonin Islands, north of what is now Iwo Jima—so Taylor's travels were in places whose names have since become familiar. South of the Bay of Yedo (Tokyo) in July, actual trade negotiations were begun. They returned to Hong Kong in August; Taylor stayed in Macao for a while and was discharged from the Navy in September. He sailed for New York on September 9, arriving there on December 20, thus ending a trip which had occupied two years and four months, and which had covered, he said, fifty thousand miles. This trip was interesting because the places were unusual. And, for the first time, Taylor lambasts those who he thinks deserve it, including those who caused him inconvenience. He complained about the Navy, he attacked the Pacific and Orient Lines, and he delivered a calm, sensible judgment of the East India Company.

He liked India, but he thought the natives too submissive. He condemned the caste system and English prejudices against Indians, "those of our own Caucasian blood, where there is no instinct of race to excuse their unjust prejudice" (273). He rode on elephants, palanquins, and every other conceivable conveyance. He noted signs of phallic worship, saying, "There is a profound philosophical truth hidden under the singular forms of this worship, if men would divest themselves for a moment of a prudery with regard to such subjects, which seems to be the affectation of the present age" (247). Indeed, he exhibited considerable religious tolerance: "There is something in every form of religion worthy of general respect." Nonetheless, his confidence in Christianity was never really shaken.

Despite his criticism of English prejudices, Taylor admired English rule. In Aden, he said, "Here on the farthest Arabian shore . . . were Law, Order, Security, Freedom of Conscience and of Speech, and all the material advantages which are insep- arable from these" (30). But he was sometimes more critical, especially of the East India Company; and occasionally he saw behind the façade. Calcutta, he said, "is a fair outside, a frontis- piece of wealth and parade, concealing the insignificance and poverty of the interior. Penetrate the thin crust, which hints of greater splendors behind it, and you are soon lost in winding, dusty avenues, lined with the mean and narrow dwellings of the lower classes of the native population" (263). He noted also the Englishman's desire to re-create his homeland wherever he was.

The Chinese filled Taylor with aversion; they had "dull faces, without expression, unless a coarse glimmering of sensuality may be called such" (285). They were ugly and filthy; even their art was bad: "The only taste which the Chinese exhibit to any degree, is a love of the monstrous" (353). In addition, they were physically inferior, exhibiting a "total want of that elegant symmetry which distinguishes the Caucasian and Shemitic races" (336). Why Taylor's distaste for the Chinese should be so violent is mysterious, but he had expressed similar opinions in California. On the other hand, he admired the Japanese, who were neat and clean, "tall, handsomely formed men, with vigorous and symmetrical bodies." Their faces "denoted a lively and active mind"; besides, they too despised the Chinese.

In Taylor's account of the American negotiations one sees the crassness of nineteenth-century commercial exploitation, but he does not regard it as such. The American emphasis on dignity, precedence, and threats shows the ugly side of the matter. Taylor, however, was jubilant that Perry had achieved in ten days what others hadn't in two hundred years. That it was achieved through a display of unmitigated arrogance and force he apparently did not realize. (This expedition was only preliminary; Perry returned the following year.) Still, Taylor's account of Japan is interesting and was probably the most valuable part of this volume.

One thing that shows clearly in this book is Taylor's propensity for making fast friends of servants, guides, and other lower-class men (he rarely mentions meeting women). He was vain about this ability, especially since his admirers were worshipful. There was Bufleb and Achmet, his Egyptian dragoman; in Spain, his guide burst into tears at the prospect of leaving him; and, on the navy ship, he quickly acquired the love of several sailors. He told George Boker that "There is room in one's heart, you know, for a score of these simple friendships, and I am restless and unhappy when I am without them."[21] He seemingly had a constant need for approval, for he not only solicited the good opinion of friends about his work but also about himself.

He feared that so much traveling had changed him, and he worried because he had not written much poetry. "I have relapsed into a traveler, an adventurer, seeking the heroic in actual life, yet without attaining it," and neglecting "the glorious art to which I once devoted myself."[22] He worried about the persistence of his thirst "for a roving, venturesome life." However, these misgivings disappeared when he returned to harness: "If God gives me life and health I shall prove that I am something better than a mere traveler,—a reputation which the world is now trying to force upon me."[23]

VI   Cyclopaedia of Modern Travel (*1856*)

Taylor also edited travel books, and the first was the *Cyclopaedia of Modern Travel*, which he began in the spring of 1855 and finished a year later. It was proposed to him by a Cincinnati publisher and sold by subscription. Taylor was interested in it chiefly for the money—he hoped to make ten thousand dollars on it in two years. However, it disappointed him financially, despite the great amount of work it had cost him—he said he had compressed ninety volumes into one. The publisher attributed its failure to the presidential elections and to "apprehensions of a financial crisis." Taylor revised it three years later to earn something more from it, but that hope was also not fulfilled.

The Cyclopaedia of Modern Travel: A Record of Adventure, Exploration, and Discovery for the Past Fifty Years: Comprising Narratives of the Most Distinguished Travelers since the beginning of this Century[24] was as massive as its title; it contained 937 double-column pages, which comprised fifty-five narratives (including one of Taylor's own); and the subject was limited to land travel. In his preface Taylor praised modern travelers as superior because more scientific and skeptical, while older travelers were more credulous. He praised the "magnificent system of colonization which is the leading feature of modern history,"[25] and he dedicated the volume to Alexander von Humboldt. An impressive work by sheer bulk, it contains so much that he could hardly have missed the best accounts. But it was a good selection, made with sense and taste, and proved that Taylor was a good editor. Its lack of success is inexplicable.

VII   Northern Travel. Summer and Winter Pictures.
      Sweden, Denmark and Lapland (*1857*)[26]

Taylor's life had by now become an alternating sequence of
roughly two years abroad and two years at home. This division
of time didn't continue forever, but it testified to his real thirst
for travel and for new experience; moreover, once successful
as a travel writer, he had to keep going. After his Eastern trip
he stayed home for two and a half years; but he did not stop
traveling. Lecturing forced him to travel a great deal, and he
was flooded with invitations. Eager to make as much as he could,
he accepted all invitations. (During 1854-55 he lectured one
hundred and thirty times, which would have earned him between
seven and ten thousand dollars.) But the pace was too much,
together with all his other work, and he broke down physically
in February, 1856. He recovered quickly, though, and returned
to the circuit after losing only a couple of weeks.

He lectured during the winter, wrote during the summer, and
in between went on other trips. In 1855 he went to Newfound-
land with a cable-laying expedition; he took his entire family
to visit Mammoth Cave; and he occasionally journeyed to Canada
to secure an English copyright. But during the summers he produced a great deal of work. He prepared three volumes from
the Eastern trip; he published *Poems of the Orient;* he prepared
a new edition of *Views A-Foot;* and he worked hard on the
Cyclopaedia. During the preparation of the last work, Taylor
became more conscious of the possibilities of travel writing, according to his wife. Impressed by his wide reading, and also
by his meeting with Humboldt, he felt "his own lack of severe
and specific training."[27] He speculated on whether there might
be "such a work as a human cosmos," whatever that means.
Whether this study resulted in improvement of his own books
remains to be seen.

By 1856 Taylor was planning a journey to the Northern countries. This time he took along his sister, a brother, and John
Braisted, a sailor he had met on the Eastern trip, as a companion-
valet. The trip is evidence of Taylor's prosperity; indeed, he
told his mother in March, 1856, that his royalties and *Tribune*
stock had paid him $5,400 for six months.[28] To this sum was
added his lecturing income and the payment for articles, stories,

and poems he constantly published in periodicals. From all sources, one might guess that his yearly income was around twenty-five thousand dollars—quite large considering the value of money at the time.

Northern Travel demonstrates that there was not much to see in the North except snow and massive scenery. Even his wife remarked that the book conveys the sense of a feat performed rather than of a pleasant journey. But Taylor wanted to experience the Far North and to compare it with the Southern latitudes of his previous trip. The trip began December 1, 1856, on a ship to Stockholm; from there he and Braisted traveled north by horse-drawn sled along the coast of the Gulf of Bothnia to Haparanda. They entered Finland and continued to their farthest northern point, about 68°, a fair distance above the Arctic Circle. They returned by the same route to Stockholm by mid-February. At this point, the book breaks in two; he went elsewhere (actually, he became engaged to Marie Hansen at this time); and, in July, the second half of the book begins.

The dominant note of the first half is, of course, the cold. Taylor minutely recorded his sensations as he moved toward the Arctic Circle; from his records, the coldest he endured was -50° F. He, of course, advises the reader what to wear, what to eat, how to keep awake, even how to drive a reindeer. He tried valiantly to describe scenery; but, since it consisted mostly of snow, its appeal is limited. He grudgingly concedes that "the Polar zone was never designed for the abode of man." He tried to point up some contrasts between South and North; extreme cold is not bracing, he said: "The tropics relax, the pole benumbs, and the practical result is the same in both cases" (160). This comment brings forth one of his more interesting speculations; one day he had a vision of the South—"A world of glorious vitality, where Death seemed an unaccountable accident. Here in the North, life existed only on sufferance, and all Nature frowned with a robber's demand to give it up" (173). But he found this thought "disturbing," and quickly dropped it, though the general comparison haunted him.

The North offered little to satisfy his thirst for experience, but he did try a Finnish vapor bath, found it bracing, and quickly accustomed himself to women attendants. This custom led him to bewail false prudery, as he had done before. He had a habit of titillating the reader, however, by suggesting that he could tell a lot more about unusual customs, except for "that morbid prudery so prevalent in our day."

Taylor liked the Swedes, "noble specimens of the physical man—tall, broad-shouldered, large-limbed, ruddy and powerful" (46). Their good health resulted in "morality and honesty," and the country people were "simple, honest, and unsophisticated." Laplanders were something else; ruined by Christianity, they had become pious and commonplace, and had lost whatever "of barbaric poetry there might have been in their composition." They hadn't even any picturesque vices.

Three things he disliked in Stockholm: the unusual conventionality, with rigid social customs; the licentiousness—scarcely one in ten shop girls was chaste, he said, though how he knew is mysterious; but he worried about their impairing the "sanctity of marriage, and . . . the general standard of morality." Finally, he was annoyed at misunderstanding of America. "There is more intellectual activity in the Free States than in any other part of the world," he asserted. "Yet this cry of 'materialism' has become the cant and slang of European talk concerning America" (225). Still, Taylor was able to express his innate optimism: the people there were, "according to their light, fully as true, and honest, and pure, as the inhabitants of the most favoured countries in the world. Love for each other, trust in each other, faith in God, are all vital among them. . . . You who spend your lives at home can never know how much good there is in the world" (162).

The second half of the book dealt with a trip along the west coast of Norway, for he wanted to see the midnight sun from the North Cape. Still accompanied by Braisted, he was joined at Oslo by Bufleb; and they set off together for Trondheim and other stops, into Varanger Fjord, their farthest north being 71° 20 minutes. Returning by much the same route, they visited various fjords and spectacular scenes on the way to Oslo. Taylor left Norway after two months, wandered through Dalecarlia, and returned to Stockholm in September.

The weather on this half of the journey was better, and the spectacular scenery gave Taylor more chances at descriptive writing. However, one fjord is much like another; therefore, the descriptions are much alike. Taylor thought the Riukan Foss the most beautiful cataract in the world, and his way of knowing it was is interesting: "I looked upon it with that involuntary suspension of the breath and quickening of the pulse, which is the surest recognition of beauty" (393).

Actually, the chief item that keeps the reader awake is Taylor's constant outrage at the Norwegians; they overcharged for everything, and he never missed a chance to lambaste them for their stupidity, ugliness, and drunkenness. They lack the "symmetrical forms and frank, friendly faces" of the Swedes. "Their carriage is awkward, and their faces not only plain but ugly." They were dirty, too, "the filthiest people in Europe. . . ." Bergen was full of venereal disease and drunkenness, and all Norway was full of illegitimate children; indeed, "no agricultural population in the world . . . stands lower in the scale of chastity," said Taylor. There were also many people with leprosy, a disease he attributed to dirtiness and immoral living.

During all these travels he had also visited Denmark: he spent three days in Copenhagen and visited with Hans Christian Andersen. With this journey Taylor satisfied his yearning to know what the cold country was like. He never returned to Scandinavia, though he some years later visited Iceland. But his considered judgment was that "the extreme North, like the Tropics, is unfavourable to the best mental and physical condition of the human race. The proper zone of man lies between 30° and 55° North" (193).

IX   Travels in Greece and Russia (*1859*)[29]

Between *Northern Travel* and *Travels in Greece and Russia*, Taylor married Marie Hansen in Gotha on October 27, 1857. Their courtship was somewhat mysterious, for Taylor hardly mentioned her before he wrote his mother that he was about to be married. She was the niece of Bufleb's wife and the daughter of an astronomer of some note. The marriage helped seal Taylor's interest in Germany and guaranteed that he would be visiting there frequently in the future. Taylor took his bride to London, where they worked together preparing *Northern Travel* for the press. Marie described his mode of working: "The text was ready to hand in the letters which he had written for the New York *Tribune* during his trip to Norway, Sweden, and Lapland, and it was only necessary to put them together and join

them into a consistent whole.... he ... allowed me to cut out
and paste the published letters on sheets of paper."[30]

Taylor now wanted to travel to Russia, but financial problems
in America made it too expensive to go either there or home, so
they spent the winter in Greece. The Greek half of *Travels in
Greece and Russia* is dominated by two themes: the racial deca-
dence of modern Greeks; and the visible remnants of the great
ages. This trip was a field day for Taylor, for Greece furnished
limitless art, architecture, and mythology to rhapsodize over.
As for real Greeks, they were extinct—though he found a few on
the slopes of Mt. Parnassus.

The trip began in December, 1857, when Taylor and his bride
sailed with Braisted to Athens. Subsequent trips consisted of
Taylor and Braisted; Marie stayed in Athens. Taylor gave much
detail about Athens life, including a Greek baptism, King Otho,
court life, and extended information on the cost of food, shelter,
and fuel. Greece lacked paved roads, and the absence of interest
in such things baffled Taylor. "There is no such thing as enterprise here," someone told him; the people were too lazy. When
he saw the palace, he said: "What avails this single flash of
imperial splendor, in a land which has not a single road, where
there is no permanent security for life and property, and whose
treasury is hopelessly bankrupt?" (65). One great impediment
to progress was the Church, which observed a holiday every
three days or so, resulting in "a general loafing-spell of the inhabitants."

The Parthenon awed him: "I was seized with an overpowering
mixture of that purest and loftiest admiration which is almost
the same thing as love" (40). As usual, he nearly threw himself "prone upon the marble pavement." In Greece, he said,
"The soul of ancient Art and Poetry throbs in the splendid air
and pours its divinest light upon the landscape" (216). But one
of Taylor's endearing qualities is that, occasionally, he saw himself posturing and was rescued by his realistic streak. On the
peak of Oeta, he confessed his only association was an absurd
one: "Let us be honest, if we cannot be ideal. When a man
always feels the proper emotion at the right place, suspect
him!" (238).

Despite the profusion of shrines, Taylor was hard put to fill the
volume; he included, therefore, stories told him by natives, even

a recipe for chicken soup, and at one point he made a paragraph into rhymes. He attacked several of his favorite topics, one of which was the "humbug," solitude: "Nature, without Man, is a sorry teacher." In summarizing, he attributed three virtues to modern Greeks: "They are remarkably chaste, for a southern race; they are probably the most temperate people in the world; and they are most unselfish and devoted in their family relations" (263). But he criticized the land, court, army, and lack of development, especially of agriculture. While the great past of Greece remained in the memory, one senses that modern Greece was something of a disappointment to Taylor.

Taylor and Marie then traveled to Constantinople, sailed up the Black Sea coast to the mouth of the Danube River; and then he took her home to Germany, after which he traveled alone to Poland and Russia. He visited Cracow and Warsaw, reverently saw the graves of Poniatowsky and Kosciusko, and descended into the great salt mines of Wieliczka. He generalized little about Poland, but he noted that the prominent characteristics of the peasants were "strength, coarseness, and stupidity, occasionally relieved by a twinkle of cunning" (290). "Better class" Polish women, however, were quite impressive, but worst of all were the Jews, "rusty, black, and unwashed." And his visit to Russia was similarly brief; most of the time in Moscow he spent visiting cathedrals, the Kremlin, markets and bazaars, and the foundling hospital. He liked Russia, and praised especially the hospital, contrasting its effectiveness with the hypocrisy of Western nations toward illegitimacy; the Russian system had not been detrimental to the general morality of the people.

The two books which came from these European journeys are among Taylor's less interesting ones. Both combine two separate journeys; and, while *Northern Travel* worked because the parts covered similar places, the second one shows no particular connection between Greece and Russia. His wife argued that the book on Greece was much better than Taylor's previous books because of the reading he had done for the *Cyclopaedia*: "The nice proportion, the composition, indeed, of his work on Greece indicate that even though he wrote necessarily in fragments, his work assumed a unity and true perspective as he went on with it."[31] However, this improvement is not readily apparent. Through his experience writing such books, *Travels in Greece*

and Russia is competently done; but, in fact, it is much like
the others. The same interests are evident—the same concern with
the annual tonnage of olives, the miles of paved road, or the
annual income of the king. On the other hand, the competence
of these books should not be underestimated. From the sopho-
moric beginnings of *Views A-Foot,* Taylor had become a professional traveler and writer about travel; and the sales of the
books suggest they must have interested many readers.

X   At Home and Abroad (*1859*)

Taylor left Hamburg with his wife and newborn daughter on
October 1, 1858, and arrived in New York on the twentieth; and
thus began one of his longest stays at home, about two and
a half years. He returned to the routine of lecturing during the
winter and of writing and supervising the building of "Cedarcroft" during the summer. Besides lecturing, he made other
domestic trips too—a three-month tour of California, for example.
However, Taylor was losing interest in travel. His wife said that
his trip to Greece had finally satisfied the impulse, "for it was not
so much a craving for knowledge of the world as it was a desire
to place himself *en rapport* with a wide range of humanity and
nature, which had given him a restlessness of life."[32] Besides,
he had now given "hostages to fortune," and he was more interested in domestic life. Certainly, his new house occupied much
time and attention (and great sums of money) during this period.

Though he did no traveling overseas, he still produced two
travel books, collections of reprinted short pieces, which are
among his more interesting works. The essays are various; several are about his American travels; a few are personal. Since
Taylor wrote no autobiography, the personal essays in *At Home
and Abroad*[33] are a source of information about his life. The
American essays include a three-part account of the trip to
Mammoth Cave, Kentucky, in 1855; it is elaborately descriptive,
though its only notable remark is "What mostly struck me in my
underground travels was the evidence of *design* which I found
everywhere." In a five-part account of his trip to Newfound-
land, which he visited in 1855, he thought the area lacked true
progressive spirit; but he met some interesting people (and dogs)
and concluded that the people had "pure, vital blood, unmixed

with any of those morbid elements which so often poison the life
of our physically and spiritually intemperate American people"
(273)—what he meant is not clear. Other pieces concern northern
New York, Canada, Mackinaw, and the Great Lakes.

Several essays deal with his first trip to England; one of the
best is "A Young Author's life in London," which recounts his
poverty in 1846, his resentment at the low-class company he was
forced to keep, and his attempts to sell an epic poem to a publisher. What one sees here is his powerful desire to be "respectable"; for, a country boy sure of his talent, he is certain he will
rise if he has a bit of luck and the right friends. In another essay,
he recounts his visits to literary shrines, referring to Shakespeare's
birthplace as "the sacred room"; of course, his impulse at the
Bard's tomb was to kneel and "kiss the dusty slab." Otherwise, he
writes about authors he visited, a form of name dropping of
which he never tired.

Seventeen pieces deal with isolated side trips during his
European journeys; most are about Germany, and they are the
dullest—a walk from Heidelberg to Nürnberg, another through
the Thuringian Forest; visits to castles, to Weimar, to the University of Jena. He also met some authors, notably Humboldt,
whom he held in great reverence. The Germans are, he said, a
"people of abstract ideas . . . given to a kind of theorizing which
breeds intellectual egotism." German conceptions are always
"based upon some abstract doctrines—theories of race, or 'national
elements'—which every year sees scattered to the winds, but,
nevertheless, they put the fragments together again, and look
upon the structure with the same unshaken complacency as before" (462)—a remark that seems ominously perceptive.

The best piece in the book and also one of his best pieces is
about the Atlantic Ocean; though only five pages long, it is finely
evocative, thoughtful, and modest. Sea travel, he said, had always
been for him a means of rest and refreshment: "The spirit of
Work infects our atmosphere: we cannot escape the malady.
Our souls are pitted and scarred with it, and there is no vac-
cination whereby we can avoid the disease. . . . There is no such
thing as rest inside of Sandy Hook. . . . Our country gives us
everything, but she exacts everything from us in return" (47).
This theme is a familiar Taylor one; harassed by the pressure
of work and the need for money, he frequently cried out against

the pressure and complained of the inability of most Americans to relax. But this essay is good writing, rhythmically fine, the kind of prose he could write when he took care: "At sea, you look on the life from which you have emerged, as one looks from a mountain top on his native town. It is astonishing how fast your prejudices relax after the land has sunk—how the great insignificances in which you have been involved, disappear, as if they had never been, and every interest of real value starts into sudden distinctness...." (50).

Two essays on supernatural experiences are curiosities. Though Taylor despised Spiritualism, he claims to have had mystical experiences of his own. One night in California he thought he heard voices in the wind singing "Vivant coelum"; another time, while staying at an inn supposedly haunted, he felt ghostly fingertips brush his forehead. Some of his experiences suggest clairvoyance, and he was interested in what today one would call extrasensory perception.

"Preferences, after Seeing the World" suggests that Americans should learn relaxation from the Germans and comfort in domestic life from the English; as for climate, he prefers California. In the United States, he says, there is no society; and life is too much dominated by a predominant religious sect in an area, the equivalent of a "religious test, which prevails to a greater extent... than in any other country in the world..." (495). However, in the last analysis, America was best because individual freedom outweighs other virtues elsewhere. He felt "well satisfied with the land where my lot is cast, without feeling myself bound to say that nothing is better elsewhere" (500)— an intelligent sort of patriotism.

The four personal essays are not greatly significant in a literary sense, but show Taylor's more human side. "The First Journey I Ever Made" concerns a trip, at eighteen, mostly walking, to New York and Catskill. "A Night Walk" tells of his trip to Washington for a passport before his first overseas trip in 1844. (He received the passport from John C. Calhoun and got to shake the hand of John Quincy Adams.) "First Difficulties with Foreign Tongues" boasts about his facility with languages, and he asserts that fifty words of a country's language is enough to get by anywhere.

At Home and Abroad is an uneven but interesting volume; one can dip into it here and there and find pleasant amusement. The author is not straining to fill five hundred pages, and so he seems easier, more informal, more modest and self-critical. Perhaps he is simply older, more judicious and tolerant.

XI At Home and Abroad, *Second Series* (1862)[34]

Between the first and second series of *At Home and Abroad,* Taylor spent most of his time lecturing and working on his new house. He wrote a friend that during 1859-60 he had lectured two hundred and seventy times in eighteen months;[35] this included a tour of California, which occupied him from August to October, 1859. Of course, while he was making a good deal of money, he was also spending a lot; for his house demanded a constant outlay of ready cash. But Civil War fever was growing, and it affected both book sales and lecture income—especially since Taylor made no attempt to conceal his Abolitionist opinions. It wouldn't have done any good, anyway, since his connection with Greeley was widely known. But his own war fever also grew; and, when his brother Frederick joined the army, Taylor sold a *Tribune* share to contribute to the war effort.

Taylor made a brief trip to Europe with his wife in the spring of 1861. They spent a few days in London, visited his wife's home in Gotha, and returned to the United States three months later. They stayed, however, only nine months; for, during his winter lecture tour, Taylor was offered the post as secretary of legation in St. Petersburg. This included a promise of becoming chargé d'affaires and the possibility of becoming minister, so he accepted the position chiefly for the steady income. He and his family left in May, 1862; he left them in Gotha and proceeded alone to St. Petersburg on June 19. His hopes for the ministership were disappointed; and, when he resigned after a year, he had hints of another post in Persia for which he waited in Gotha until July, 1863. But, hearing of his brother's death at the battle of Gettysburg, he returned home in September, 1863.

The Second Series is much like the first in kind and quantity of material. There was a German section, including a ten-part article about a home in the Thuringian Forest, and a long essay about a hike through Franconian Switzerland. There was a large American section, including a ten-part article on California that

filled one hundred and sixty-five pages; and the account of a trip
he made with Bufleb through New York State and New England
filled eighty-four pages. There were also four personal essays
about building his house, five accounts of visits to authors, and—
oddly enough—two short stories. The walking trip essay recounts
a return to that mode in Switzerland in an attempt to strengthen
his knees that were, he said, weak from riding in American rail-
way carriages. (Since he was tall, he suffered from accommoda-
tions designed for the average man.) It is a pleasant, though not
significant, essay with much scenery description.

During July, 1861, Taylor rented a cottage in the Thuringian
Forest, near Friedrichsroda. He asserted that the ideal kind of
travel was to study men in their homes, "*from* a home among
them"; but this laudable idea he seldom followed. He added:
"With a little human flexibility, a catholic breadth of taste, and
an entire freedom from the prejudices of the Little Pedlington in
which most men are born, we may, without sacrificing a jot of
our individuality, without hazarding the loss of a single principle, live the life of other races and other climates, and thus
gather into our own the aggregate experience of Man" (205).
He interpreted German history and legends, described the
forest culture of Germany, and dined with the Duke of
Saxe-Coburg-Gotha.

One new element in these essays, however, is his patriotic
outbursts about the Civil War. He regarded himself as the
interpreter of the struggle to the Germans; in Europe, he said,
"it is our republican form of government that is on trial." He
prayed that God would preserve us "from the shame, the ineradi-
cable infamy of Peace on any other terms than the unconditional
submission of the traitors!" (209). He apparently received a
sympathetic audience from Germans, one of whose basic desires
was their own unification. The most interesting thing about this
essay, however, is that near its end he became suddenly more
personal, complaining again about the American drive for success. At times he sounds like Thoreau: "Why should we not regu-
late our lives in accordance with the common sense of our own
natures, whether or not it chimes in with the common sense of
the world? On every side we see blossoms that only seem to
wait for our plucking; every wind brings us their betraying
odors; yet we turn away, and go on with our old business of

pulling thistles, no matter how our hands bleed. A great portion of our lives is spent in achieving something that we do not actually need" (279-80).

Such remarks reflect moments of self-doubt, or wonder about whether or not the game is worth the effort. "An author writes, generally," he said, "from the dearth of that which he desires: where life gives it to him in overflowing measure, he enjoys and is silent" (271). Why not then simply enjoy life, "make life itself your art and your passion?" This question is, of course, the right one; but his only answer is, "Because I cannot. Give me means, time, freedom from restraining ties—still I cannot. Leave the Christian idea of Duty out of sight . . . still, we are so constituted that our truest enjoyment comes through the force of contrast. . . . Why should I not sit, with folded hands, and be satisfied with feeling these thoughts lazily ripple along the shores of the mind, instead of grappling with language, and achieving, at best, an imperfect expression? Because the struggle is necessary, in order to give coherent shape to thought" (282). And so he left his cottage willingly, knowing what was ahead, knowing that for him there was no real alternative. "I hear, already, the grating of the upper and nether mill-stones of everyday life, and prepare to jump into the hopper" (283).

The account of the summer trip with Bufleb is one of his best pieces. He admitted not having written much about America, but he thought it a good thing "not to see all your own country until after you have seen other lands." They went up the Hudson River by boat, then through western Massachusetts to Pittsfield and Boston. His friend thought Massachusetts soil looked barren; Taylor replied that people praise rather "her laws, her school system, her morals, and her men!" Taylor's remarks on Boston are amusing; and, in a strange way, they foreshadow those of later writers. "A Boston Sunday, in winter," he began, "is a day of sack-cloth and ashes. A foreigner would suppose there was weekly fasting and prayer for some great national calamity" (337-8). In a remark that reminds one of Scott Fitzgerald, he said: "The genuine Bostonian . . . hopes that he will go to Paris when he dies" (340). Another passage recalls one by George Santayana: "I have sometimes wondered whether all the Bostonians postpone their Parisian delights until after death. Is there nothing volcanic under this cold lava. No indulgence in

improprieties, all the more attractive, because secret?" (340).
While it is now standard procedure to poke fun at Boston, it was
not so common in Taylor's time; indeed, he was usually more
circumspect about the pretensions of Bostonians when he wanted
their approval; but his joking about them shows how far he had
come in self-confidence.

The trip to California is quite interesting; but, when *Eldorado*
was reprinted in 1949, this second trip was apparently overlooked. It was exactly ten years later that Taylor arrived with
his wife in San Francisco, now a city of eighty thousand, after
he had been invited by a literary society to make a lecture tour
from which he expected to make five thousand dollars in three
months, though he made barely half that. San Francisco society
he thought refined and cultivated; "its tone is liberal and metro-
politan and the mingling of so many various elements relieves it
of that prim, respectable dullness which characterizes some of
our older cities" (48). His lectures were well attended, the
audiences receptive and well behaved. Most of the lectures, however, were in small towns—San Jose, Petaluma, Santa Rosa, Napa
City, and Sacramento (where the audience was less polite: some
members went out for a drink in the middle of this lecture).
Taylor's farm background caused him to be impressed by monstrous vegetables: he saw pumpkins that weighed two hundred
and sixty pounds, and a beet of one hundred and fifteen pounds.
"And then comes the question—if plants change, wherefore not
men? And if so, how? Or is the change only in the hidden roots
of our character, not in the boughs and blossoms which we
show to the world?" (118). He imagined the San Joaquin Valley
a century later, filled with the "wild magnificence of Nature . . .
humming with human life" and with art, culture, plenty, peace,
and happiness everywhere.

There was, however, a small note of doubt. "The Californians
have labored well, it is true, but not so much as they might
have done. . . . The *energy of Selfishness* has worked wonders—
but it takes something more to make a State great, wise, and
happy" (62). When he considered California as a place to live,
he admitted that, first, it was beautiful; second, it was "free,
liberal, sensible"; third, the climate was the same as Andalusia
and Sicily; fourth, the air was unusually pure (this will no
doubt surprise present residents); and, finally, the wine was very

good. On the whole, he said, it was a land "where life seems to
be most plastic . . . one may shape his existence in the most
various molds." But, if all this is true, "Why not, then, escape
care, consumption, cold, neuralgia, fashion, bigotry, eastwinds,
gossip, and chilblains, and fly to that happy shore? For one simple reason: It is *too new*—too recently fallen into the possession
of man—too little touched, as yet, with the genial influences of
Art and Taste. Life, at present, is beautiful there, but lonely;
and so it must remain for another generation to come" (200).

The essays about building "Cedarcroft" are among Taylor's
best informal prose—pleasant, cheerful, witty, and unpretentious.
The first argues that his desire to own land was hereditary and
that "one cannot properly be considered as a member of the
Brotherhood of Man" until he possesses a portion of earth's surface. In "Free Soil," he lists his requirements for guests: they
may wear what they choose, and thought and speech shall be
free (unnecessary profanity excepted). Not admissable are
"hypocritical, insincere, time-serving creatures, shams of all
kinds, men with creaking boots, stealthy cat-step, oily faces,
and large soft hands" (15)—plus reformers, worshippers of the
golden calf, and bores.

The third essay deals with actual problems of building a house,
and its most notable point is that (in 1859) they don't build
them as they used to. The last essay concentrates on landscape
gardening, particularly on trees, of which Taylor was very fond.

At Home and Abroad, Second Series, is, all in all, probably
Taylor's best travel book; it is certainly one of his best prose
works. Not only is there more American material in it, but the
European material is handled with a defter hand and with
greater ease. Generally, the essays are more serious and thoughtful, at the same time that they are less forced and more witty;
and the writing is more careful than usual. The two short stories
and the visits to authors are trivial; but the rest of the book contains some of his best writing.

XII   Colorado: A Summer Trip (*1867*)[36]

Taylor's diminishing interest in travel is suggested by the fact
that, after his return from Russia in 1863, he did not go to Europe
again until 1867, a comparatively long term. Nor did he produce

a book from his year in Russia, despite his wife's claim that one
motive in going there was to write a major work of travel about
the almost unknown interior of the country. "Exploring Central
Asia, under Russian protection," he wrote the Stoddards, sur-
prisingly, "was the great ambition" of his life.[37]

During this time, Taylor settled down to his usual routine—
New York in the winter, "Cedarcroft" in the summer, and frequent trips here and there. He produced a good deal: three
novels, a collected edition of his poems, and what he thought was
one of his best narrative poems, *The Picture of St. John.* He also
worked on his translation of *Faust.* It might be noted that on
January 11, 1865, Taylor was forty years old; and it seems
amazing that a man who had done so much, been so many places,
and published some twenty books was only now reaching forty;
but one remarkable thing about Taylor's career is that it began
so very early.

During June and July, 1866, Taylor made a trip to the Colorado Territory as a sort of vacation; but he also wrote letters to
the *Tribune* and lectured in Colorado towns. He went, he said,
because he felt "the want of new scenes: the old craving for a
change of external experience comes back—my physical cosmos
is not yet completed, it seems." The resultant volume is a
slender one of only one hundred and eighty-five pages; and,
while not one of his most exciting books, its value was in being
one of the earliest accounts of the area. In some ways it reminds
one of Twain's *Roughing It* with the humor removed. It is
entirely factual, with descriptions of towns, landscapes, and
agricultural prospects, almost as if it were designed for potential
emigrants back East.

Most of the book describes journeys on horseback, camping in
the mountain country around Denver—he covered four hundred
miles this way, he said. This kind of travel Taylor liked; he enjoyed riding horses, and he liked mountain scenery. His nature
responded to grandeur, and he encountered in the Rockies as
much grandeur as one could find. His company toiled up some
high passes, and saw vast stretches of beautiful, uninhabited
land. He appreciated a freshly caught mountain trout, or venison
or bear meat—he thought the flesh of the Rocky Mountain goat
was delicious. The dominant note, however, is scenery, which he
looked at with a painter's eye.

He said little about his lecturing, except that at nine thousand feet a lecture was followed by complete exhaustion. Audiences were good; for "calm, steady attention" they might have been in New York or New England. What amazed him most, however, was the presence of social graces. "The degree of refinement which I have found in the remote mining districts of Colorado has been a great surprise," he said. "It is only the *half*-cultivated who, under such circumstances, relapse toward barbarism" (131). Generally, he thought his trip to Colorado "refreshing." He was glad he had gone when he did, "while there are still buffaloes and danger of Indians on the Plains," and while much of the country was unspoiled.

He knew it would soon be settled, civilized, and less interesting. "No one of us will live to see the beauty and prosperity which these States, even in their rude, embryonic condition, already suggest. The American of to-day must find his enjoyment in anticipating the future. He must look beyond the unsightly beginnings of civilization, and prefigure the state of things a century hence, when the Republic will count a population of two hundred millions, and there shall be leisure for Taste and Art" (184). The confidence and the prophetic accuracy of this passage are notable, and his prediction of two hundred million inhabitants by 1966 was only slightly off the mark.

It is sad that Taylor gave so little serious attention as an artist to his travel works. He told a friend that this book would probably be published "for temporary circulation (I am aware that such things have a very temporary value)."[38] Partly, he exaggerated in the way one does when he doesn't want others to think he really thinks something is good; and he certainly realized that his fame and income depended more on travel than on anything else. Although he did take some care with these books, his usual attitude is shown in a letter to Stedman about the poem, *St. John,* which he hoped would "achieve for me what I am thirsting for—recognition as a real poet."[39]

XIII   By-Ways of Europe   (*1869*)[40]

Colorado was published in January, 1867; the next month Taylor left on a European trip that lasted until nearly the end of 1868. He felt he needed a vacation: "Oh, how I long for the rest and

recreation of Europe! I confess to feeling fagged and weary, to
a mighty craving for fresh woods and pastures new.... My blood
is thick and sluggish; I sleep badly, for the first time in my
life, and have a general sense of discomfort, though I can't
put my finger on one ailing spot."[41] Nonetheless, he contracted
to write letters for the *Tribune* and articles for *The Atlantic
Monthly.*

In England, Taylor was entertained by literary society, a form
of ego-salving that did him much good. "I have made myself a
footing in England, in the last four or five years," he said
happily.[43] He made a long visit to Tennyson at Farringford, and
he gave an amazing picture of everyone (including Tennyson)
weeping with emotion during a reading by Tennyson of the
idyl of Guinevere.[42] He traveled around Europe with his family,
spending the rest of the summer in the cottage at Friedrichsroda.
In the winter, they went to Italy, where, in the Casa Guidi, he
was stricken with a serious illness from which he nearly died.
(During this illness he thought he was visited by the ghost of
Elizabeth Barrett Browning.)[44] More traveling in the Mediter-
ranean area followed before his return to Gotha, to England, and
then to New York in September, 1868.

In March, 1869, Taylor published *By-Ways of Europe,* a collection of short pieces written during the trip and first published in
the *Atlantic* or in the *Tribune.* There are only sixteen, longer
than usual; but most are about little-visited places which, he
said, "attracted me by some picturesque interest, either of history, or scenery, or popular institutions and customs." Three of
the essays reflect his Russian experiences. "A Cruise on Lake
Ladoga" describes one of the largest and least-visited lakes in
Europe. "Between Europe and Asia" narrates Taylor's visit to
a fair at Nijni-Novgorod; and "Winter Life in St. Petersburg" is
an account of ice-sledding, court balls, and the breakup of ice
on the Neva in spring. His observations of Russian landscapes
and customs are reasonably interesting; he saw *Macbeth* performed by an American Negro, met Richard Wagner and Rubin-
stein, and discovered that the Empress was fond of Longfellow.

Four essays cover Spanish material. "From Perpignan to Mont-
serrat" concerns a trip to Barcelona and the Pyrenees, including
a visit to a mountain and a monastery. "Balearic Days," in two
parts, deals with the islands of Majorca and Minorca. Spain and

Italy always evoke from Taylor a conventional anti-Catholicism; and, while he praised the natives of Majorca, he saw little chance for them to modernize under the "combined shadow of Spain and Rome." In "Bridle Roads of Catalonia" he describes his horseback trip through mountainous country from Cardona to Andorra, and he makes occasional comments on peasant life.

Four essays describe islands off Italy. On Capri, the Green Grotto evoked some of his purplest prose: "It was an idyl of the sea, born of the god-lore of Greece. To the light, lisping whisper of the waves,—the sound nearest to that of a kiss,—there was added a deep, dim, subdued undertone of the swell caught in lower arches beyond . . ." (363). "A Trip to Ischia" illustrates one fault of these pieces: the insertion of large swatches of history which occupy most of the space and suggest that Taylor hadn't much to say. "The Land of Paoli," about Corsica, consists mostly of a history of the Paoli family.

However, "The Island of Maddalena, with a distant view of Caprera" is one of the unintentionally funniest essays he ever wrote. Wanting to visit Garibaldi, Taylor sent a messenger with letters of introduction: to Taylor's outrage, Garibaldi refused to meet him, alleging illness (though Taylor could see him puttering in the garden). He sent a second note, with the same result, and gave up, complaining that the "manner in which my application had been received still appeared to me very rude and boorish." Still, he had to write an article, so he described Caprera from a distance and included a long account of Garibaldi's revolutionary activities. It is a demonstration that writing about a "non-event" was not an invention of the twentieth century.

Taylor thought *By-Ways of Europe* "much better in style and richer in substance" than his previous books. Certainly his style is polished and professional, but the format and the content of the essays are much as usual. Usually, he described the history and the government of a place, then gave some details about life there with an emphasis on agriculture. Description of the landscape, anecdotes about what happened to him there, some account of the cost of traveling complete his picture—material which is more informative than anything else.

By far the most interesting piece in this volume, however, is its preface, in which he swears off traveling. This curious piece explains how he started traveling in the first place—accidentally,

he says; circumstances forced him into it, rather than any "roving propensity" (he feels moved to deny such propensities). It
was not until his Eastern trip that he learned to feel the "passions
of the Explorer." His subsequent popularity misled him about the
work he was "best fitted to do"; and he realized that his travel
books fall short of "real achievement." In reading for the anthol-
ogy of travel, he had discovered he lacked the formal training
(in anthropology and ethnology) that marks the best travel
writing; besides, his time did not permit frankness. Thus, he
concluded he did not want to be a travel writer; *Northern
Travel* and *Greece and Russia* marked the "receding waves"
of his interest.

While he would have liked to visit Central Asia and South
America, he felt the "demoralizing influence of travel," which
he defined as the need to maintain a constant receptivity of
mind, the lack of time to assimilate, a general superficiality,
and a desultory habit of mind. He then offers an interesting
definition of two basic kinds of travel books:

The most interesting narrative of exploration is that which is most
simply told. A poetic apprehension of Nature, a sparkling humor,
graces of style—all these are doubtful merits. We want the naked
truth, without even a fig-leaf of fancy. We may not appreciate all
the facts of science which the explorer has collected, but to omit
them would be to weaken his authority. Narratives of travel serve
either to measure our knowledge of other lands, in which case they
stand only until superseded by more thorough research, or to exhibit
the coloring which those lands take when painted for us by individual
minds, in which case their value must be fixed by the common
standards of literature. For the former class, the widest scientific
culture is demanded; for the latter, something of the grace and
freedom and keen mental insight which we require in a work
of fiction. (16)

This remarkable passage explains a good deal about Taylor's
problem; one can see his dilemma was genuine. Lacking scientific training, he could not produce substantial works; yet he
did not want to write "poetic" works because his real interest
was poetry itself. His own ideal was "the naked truth"; but, in
trying to tell it, he often presented a dull collection of facts. Yet
he could not stop, for the books constituted his main source of

income, and he was clearly trapped. He confessed that being called the "great American traveler" humiliated him, for he knew his books were little more than studies of his own education. He said that he didn't want to renounce future chances entirely, but he promised he would no longer travel "from the mere desire of travel." And he invited his readers to join him in "other walks of literature" to which he now wanted to devote himself. *By-Ways of Europe,* however, was *not* his last travel book.

In its way, Taylor's declaration of independence from travel was very courageous. As has been previously observed, Taylor was finally abandoning what he did not want to do, despite the loss of income and the probable decline in living comfort. He had rethought his values, and he had found that luxurious living was not necessary and that writing poetry and turning out good work was more important to him. Significantly, he was at this time trying to sell "Cedarcroft" and was spending most of his time in New York. It should also be noted that he was finishing his translation of *Faust,* an activity that convinced him that what he wanted to do was the right thing.

XIV   Egypt and Iceland in the Year 1874 (*1874*)[45]

During the fall of 1868, Taylor refused to lecture, devoting himself instead to literary work, of which he produced a good deal. He worked on *By-Ways,* on his last novel *Joseph and His Friend,* published many individual poems, and read some public verse; he also became nonresident professor of German literature at Cornell University, conducted a monthly chronicle of literature and art for *Putnam's Magazine,* and wrote frequent reviews and criticism for the *Tribune.* In addition, he completed the first draft of the *Faust* translation in May, 1869.

But economic conditions worsened, and he was forced during 1869 to return to lecturing, though he lost money at it. "I get next to nothing from my books now," he wrote a friend in 1870; "... We are just now feeling the inevitable demoralization of the war."[46] Desperately, he agreed to another California tour, but it was a disaster; he returned early, saying "the population in California is the deadest I ever saw."[47]

Faust, Part I, was published in December, 1870, and Part II in

March, 1871. He hoped it would establish his literary and scholarly reputation, and its publication in a binding uniform with
Longfellow's *Dante* and Bryant's *Homer* was, he thought, a sign
of success. He then turned to reading and gathering material
for a combined biography of Goethe and Schiller, which he was
destined not to complete.

In June, 1872, when he sailed again for Europe to gather
material, he received a steady stream of bad news from home.
Horace Greeley, after an unsuccessful bid for the presidency,
abruptly died; and Taylor not only mourned a friend but worried
about the possible collapse of the *Tribune* in which he had
invested all his money. The paper survived under Whitelaw
Reid, but Taylor's shares never paid another dividend. He had
trouble with the tenant of his house; payments for his writing
mysteriously didn't arrive, and in November he wrote a friend
that his "whole worldly wealth at this moment consists of fifteen
groshen!"[48] A series of travel books he was editing for Scribner
was canceled; and a school history of Germany he was writing
for Appleton was long delayed—it finally appeared, but the book
earned him nothing.

He went back, perforce, to work for the *Tribune* and reported
for it the Vienna exhibition of 1873. He wanted to visit Egypt
again, and offered to write letters for Reid, who accepted. Delayed by illness in the family, Taylor spent only a month there
with Marie. When he returned to Gotha, Reid proposed that he
go to Iceland for its one thousandth anniversary—a trip that
took him about three weeks. Nonetheless, during this time he
also wrote two long poems, *Lars* and *The Prophet*. He returned
to America in September, 1874.

Egypt and Iceland consists, then, of the accounts of two brief
trips. Of all the places he had visited, he seemed to like Egypt
best, though it had been twenty-two years since his last trip
there. Thus his chief interest was modernization and "what cor-
responding change has taken place in the condition, the habits,
and the ideas of the people." He quickly discovered that "oriental repose had not yet been seriously shaken." The pyramids
still impressed him, but he made no attempt to climb them.
Their existence showed, however, the need for "a new chronol-
ogy of man," a change that would show "the unspeakable
grandeur of the Divine Soul by which it is directed." He feared

such remarks would bring on him the wrath of Mark Twain "and all others who distrust earnest impressions" (52).

He sympathized with the people: "Alas, for the Orientals! They get but scanty justice, I fear, even from us: we praise the rulers who keep them abject and ignorant, and then revile the people because they are not manly and intelligent" (90). He thought the Khedive intelligent and determined to modernize Egypt. Generally, much of Taylor's liking for the Arabs persisted, and he had doubts about Westernization. "Orientals draw comfort and strength from other sources than we do," he commented.

The Iceland half of the book is dull. Apparently the visit of Christian IX of Denmark to the millennial celebration of Iceland was a newsworthy event. Remarking that the *Tribune's* call was "like that of the trumpet unto the warhorse," Taylor was soon on a ship plowing the sea toward Iceland. Reykjavik had, he said, broad, clean streets; cosy and pleasant homes; and "truly grand" mountains; but the people had "stoical, indifferent" faces. At a banquet, Taylor read a poem of his own giving greetings from America to Iceland. This poem was immediately translated orally, and it was followed by cheers for Taylor, the Skald. He visited the geysers and Thingvalla, reported the national festival, passed on considerable history, and analyzed the new constitution. He was shortly after back in Edinburgh with the conclusion that the Icelanders were "a grand and true-hearted people."

This book represents the petering out of Taylor's travel impulse. The Iceland portion is uninspired; the Egyptian part might have been better if he had stayed longer, though it has some good parts. But, since this publication was his last travel book, it is too bad his farewell could not have been more enticing.

XV *Other Travel Works*

Even the mass of material so far described does not, however, exhaust Taylor's travel work. Many short essays, never collected, remain embalmed in the pages of the *Tribune* and other journals. Although his wife published several posthumous volumes, she never collected the travel essays, except for two pieces on

Weimar. At least a couple of volumes could be compiled from
these shorter essays.

In his later years, Taylor edited some travel books. One of
them, which is still fun to browse through, is *Picturesque Europe*:
Delineations by Pen and Pencil of the Natural Features and the
Picturesque and Historical Places of Great Britain and the Conti-
nent, published by Appleton in several enormous volumes in
1877. These books were lavishly illustrated with steel and wood
engravings, and the prose sections were taken from various un-
identified writers. The pictures are well worth the price, however, and anyone finding this set today would be fortunate.

One remaining work is Scribner's "Illustrated Library of
Travel," supposedly edited by Taylor. He began to edit it in
1871 with *Travels in Arabia*, and a year later Scribner suspended
the series. It must have been resumed, however, for five volumes
carry the notation "compiled and arranged by Bayard Taylor."
The other four are: *Japan in Our Day* (1872); *Travels in South*
Africa (1872); *The Lake Regions of Central Africa* (1873); and
Central Asia (1874). The other volumes in the series were not
prepared by Taylor, and it is difficult to know exactly how much
work he did on these five since neither he nor his wife said anything about them.

There is little to add to this account of Taylor's travel books.
They were one of his chief sources of support and fame, but
his attitude toward them much of the time was casual, sloppy,
even contemptuous. They were very uneven, the weakest ones
being *Greece and Russia* and *Egypt and Iceland*. He did not break
new ground in the travel genre; he followed standard models.
He followed taste rather than formed it, and he would not occupy
a very large place in the history of the genre were it not for the
great popularity his books enjoyed in his own era.

Yet some of these books are good, despite Taylor's uncertain
attitudes. The truth is that the quality of a given book depended
on his situation at the time—whether he needed money, had a
short deadline, or was preoccupied with other things. There was
a point, as has been said, when he saw possibilities in the genre;
and, although he could not finally do anything about developing
it, he did take pains with some of these books. *Views A-Foot*
was not a very good book, but it is interesting because of its
novelty and youthful enthusiasm. *Central Africa* has some good

description and observation; at times, one feels attracted to the exotic scene. The short personal pieces, really informal essays, are pretty good pieces of prose; and *At Home and Abroad*, I and II, are probably his most interesting volumes. These and *Eldorado* are his best works in the genre; the former, for their variety; the latter, for its vitality and sharp observation. All these books have some historical interest, but *Eldorado* is already a small classic of Westerniana. Indeed, while Taylor spent most of his time writing for Americans about the rest of the world, he seems most interesting when he wrote about America; and one regrets that he did not do more things like *Eldorado, Colorado*, or his many short essays on American places.

Taylor fulfilled the need of Americans of his time for news of the outside world, and he did so reasonably well. His books are informative, anecdotal, and communicate some sense of the life he saw. If they now seem sometimes dull, it is because one's familiarity with the world is greater, one's attitudes about what is important are different, and one's demands are higher. He answered the demands of his own day successfully; and, if his travel books are not really for the ages, it is only fair to say that he never intended them to be.

CHAPTER 3

Fiction

FROM 1861 to 1869 Taylor wrote novels. Since he had turned his hand so readily to every type of literary activity, his attempt with this genre should not be surprising. Moreover, one must remember that he was a professional writer, living on what he earned with his pen; consequently, he developed a sharp eye for activities that promised a reasonable return for his labors. The novel had grown in popularity in the first half of the nineteenth century, and the financial success of Charles Dickens and others seemed to promise great reward if one could find the proper combination of qualities to appeal to a large audience. The most important reason for Taylor to turn to fiction, however, was the decline of his lecturing during the Civil War. He still lectured during these years, and some years were better than others; but his income from this activity declined sharply, and, in casting about for other sources, he hit on the novel. He still produced a good deal of other writing, and he worked intensively in the later years on the translation of *Faust.* Indeed, the melancholy part of Taylor's story is that he was constantly too busy, too pressed by deadlines, too harrassed to do as good a job on anything as he could have done.

Taylor wrote four novels: *Hannah Thurston* (1863); *John Godfrey's Fortunes* (1864); *The Story of Kennett* (1866); and *Joseph and His Friend* (1870). In addition, he collected some short stories into a volume, published in 1872 as *Beauty and the Beast and Tales of Home.*[1] These novels are not notable for their technical interest; for, although Taylor quickly mastered the needed skills of fiction writing, he didn't make any innovations. The books are straightforward in organization and structure. They are loosely yet elaborately plotted in the manner of Dickens. Frequently melodramatic, they contain many confrontations and

76

verbal duels in which the hero defends right, justice, or beauty
in ringing tones while the villain slinks ignominiously away.
They also embody the nineteenth-century conception of good
and evil—the belief that there are good and evil men, that good
is easily recognizable, and that people who become involved in
evil are being perverse, are corrupted by bad examples, and
so forth.

I   Hannah Thurston (*1863*)

Taylor's first venture with the novel was begun in midwinter
of 1861, but *Hannah Thurston* was not published until November, 1863, because a great many things interrupted the writing
of it, chief of which was his tenure as Secretary of Legation in
St. Petersburg. In his preface, Taylor said that he had uncovered
some new material, an area of American life overlooked by previous novelists: "I perceived peculiarities of development in
American life which have escaped the notice of novelists, yet
which are strikingly adapted to the purposes of fiction, both in
the originality and occasional grotesqueness of their external
manifestation, and the deeper questions which lie beneath the
surface. I do not, therefore, rest the interest of the book on its
slender plot, but on the fidelity with which it represents certain
types of character and phases of society" (4).

This discovery by Taylor appears to refer to the profusion of
reform movements in America, of which there were quite a
number. However, he centers his book on women's rights; and
it is difficult to see how he could have imagined that such a question had escaped the notice of writers since there had been
many treatments of the theme before this. Hawthorne's *Blithe-
dale Romance* preceded this book by not a great stretch of time;
and there was the most famous contemporary treatment of
women's rights, Tennyson's *The Princess* (1847). In fact, Tennyson's poem is usually cited as the model for *Hannah Thurston;*
Taylor's biographer, Smyth, calls the novel a prose parallel of
it,[2] and Beatty agreed that there were many similarities. Indeed,
a close examination may prove instructive about the extent of
Taylor's imagination as a novelist.

The action of the novel begins in November, 1852, in Ptolemy,
New York; an amalgamated ladies' sewing union has been

formed from several reform groups; and among those at the
union meeting is Hannah Thurston, an intelligent, strong-minded
woman who lectures on women's rights. The conversation is about
Lakeside, a local house sold to a rich Mr. Maxwell Woodbury;
he soon appears, a man of thirty-six who has been in India for
years. He is attracted by Hannah's sincerity but repelled by the
general atmosphere of reform; for he has learned repose and
tolerance in the Orient.

At the next union meeting Woodbury banters Hannah about
the idea of women's dissecting male corpses in medical school.
She defends the idea and can't understand his apparent frivo-
lousness. At one point Woodbury talks of his youth in New York
and of how he was "saved" by a Miss Remington. Meanwhile,
Hannah's mother advises her about love by telling her about her
father and their marriage; Quakerism had led to repression of
feeling, and they had both missed much happiness.

Woodbury obviously desires a wife but is both attracted and
repelled by Hannah. Once, at a picnic, when Max rescues a child
who has fallen into the river, he is himself saved by quick-
thinking Hannah. On a trip to Niagara, Max again meets Miss
Remington, now Mrs. Blake with a family; and he invites her to
Lakeside. When she comes (she's an example of the properly
balanced woman), she gives Hannah a difficult time about her
opinions. Max resolves, however, to try cultivating Hannah; he
visits her home frequently and lends her books. One day, while
walking in the woods, he confesses his feelings for her; and he
later writes her a long letter explaining his life and previous
love affairs. She is upset but impressed by his honesty and no-
bility. Finally, he declares himself; and, though she fights bitterly, he finally conquers. Hannah's mother is delighted, and
they are married a few days later.

During the early months of their marriage, Woodbury slowly
asserts himself; and Hannah's subjection increases. When she
asks him to smoke a cigar, one recognizes that she is nearly
converted. When she is asked to speak at a women's rights convention, she sends Max instead, who lectures on the real nature
of women. Hannah and Max reach marital perfection when a
baby is born; he weeps over it in a closing scene of the sheerest
sentimentality.

The similarity of this novel to *The Princess* is not very great.

True, Taylor was an avid admirer of Tennyson, and at one point the hero gives Hannah a copy of the poem in his campaign to convert her to good sense—to see woman's true role. The chief resemblance lies in the idea that a woman, who is fiercely committed to women's rights, is eventually brought low by a lover who convinces her that love and marriage are better suited to the nature of women than any amount of voting. Aside from this resemblance, there are only two specific devices that correspond: a rescue from drowning, and an illness through which, by nursing him, the woman realizes her love for the man.

Much more striking are the similarities to Jane Austen's *Pride and Prejudice*. Both books, gently satiric comedies of manners, consist of quiet incidents at teas, afternoon visits, or walks in the country. Both major characters are intensely proud and are prejudiced against what they think the other represents; and bringing such a pair to fall in love is a conventional novelistic device. There is a seduction among the minor characters; and Woodbury himself feels impelled to write a long letter, like Darcy, to justify himself. Even Taylor's style is similar; but it is, of course, not so good as Austen's.

Some of Taylor's satire is funny, but none is specific enough to offend particular groups. Mrs. Waldo, for instance, is described as "the oleaginous solvent, in which the hard yolk of the Mission Fund, the vinegar of the Cimmerians, and the mustard of the Abolitionists lost their repellant qualities and blended into a smooth social compound" (12). Mr. Grindle, on the other hand, represents "The manners which self-constituted teachers of morality must necessarily assume in a community where intellect is characterized by activity rather than development. Society, in its broader sense, is unknown to these people. . . . In the absence of cultivation, they are ruled by popular ideas: Reforms are marshalled in, as reserve corps, behind the ranks of Religion, and not even the white flag of a neutral is recognized in the grand crusade. 'Join us and establish your respectability, or resist us and be cut down!' is the cry" (103).

The book sold more than fifteen thousand copies in four months; two years later Taylor said it was still selling "at a surprising rate" and "the booksellers tell me that it already has the character of a standard work."[3] There were some unfavorable reviews, but the chief objection was that the attack on

religious reformers was unkind. But most readers liked it, and—
always important to Taylor—his literary friends praised it. Nathaniel Hawthorne, amazingly enough, wrote him: "The book is
an admirable one, new, true, and striking,—worthy of such a
world-wide observer as yourself, and with a kind of thought in
it which does not lie scattered about the world's highways."[4]
Lowell, Whittier, and others congratulated him; and Taylor
boasted that "women readers are amazed at my knowledge of
the female heart and nature." It was successful, said his wife,
with those people "who read a novel for what it may betray
of human life."[5]

On the other hand, "the critics and those who look more nar-
rowly . . . were divided."[6] Smyth argued that the book's "crudities
of style and infirmities of construction" were due to the "tearing
speed" at which it was written.[7] But, in fact, the book is not badly
constructed; and in its use of thematic repetition it is quite successful—there were several lesser love affairs to illustrate to Hannah the nature of true and false love.

However, the plot is somewhat feeble, because it is heavily
dependent on coincidence. Woodbury happens to encounter
Hannah a remarkable number of times, even in the next town.
Furthermore, some scenes have no function; they exist simply
to satirize reformers. Taylor was praised for inventing a heroine
past her first youth, and this was unusual. Indeed, as he looked
back on Hannah years later, he defended her and the book:
"Artistically, it is not a failure. To be sure, it has serious faults:
it lacks movement, especially in the first half; there is much unnecessary detail, frequently a want of relief, and some of the
characters are imperfectly developed. But Hannah Thurston, the
woman, is a successful creation; the scope and plan of the book
are correct. Were I to write it again, I would retain these as
they are. . . ."[8]

And Taylor is right in this respect; Hannah is a successful
characterization of an intelligent, independent-minded, courageous woman; and the reader is attracted to her despite such
descriptions as "no tongue dared to whisper an insinuation
against either her sincerity or her purity." Similarly, her situation,
that of intelligence lost in a backwater society, is moving; and
Taylor, at his best, makes her plight understood, as when he
describes her feelings after rejecting the proposal of Seth

Wattles, a man of profound mediocrity: "It was a most bitter, humiliating thought. With her head drooping wearily towards her breast, and her hands clasped in her lap, with unheeded tears streaming from her eyes, she sought refuge from this pain in that other pain of the imagined love that once seemed so near and lovely—lovelier now, as she saw it through the mist of a gathering despair. Thus she sat, once more the helpless captive of her dreams, while the lamp burned low and the room grew cold" (154).

The difficulty is that one likes Hannah so much that one regrets her subservience to Maxwell Woodbury, who is self-righteous and pretentious, though he is not meant to be. He tells Hannah that "a sense of reliance on the one hand and protection on the other constitutes a firmer and tenderer form of union than if the natures were evenly balanced. It is not a question of superiority, but of radical and necessary difference of nature. Woman is too finely organized for the hard, coarse business of the world, and it is for her sake that man desires to save her from it.... He stands between her and human nature in the rough..." (254). Where could one find a more accurate statement of the Genteel attitude toward relations between the sexes? Max argues that men lack "that finer protecting instinct which holds woman back from the rude, material aspects of human nature" (255). A man who talks in this fashion can hardly be taken seriously. Woodbury has faded with time, and the values that he represents; but Taylor struck in Hannah some universal chord that has kept her alive. In Woodbury's arrogant superiority and condescension, his habit of putting everybody down, he seems a pompous fool; and one feels that Hannah deserved better.

One great flaw in the book is the melodrama, an excessive reaction to events. Woodbury's impulse to thrash villains, for example, seems time-worn though it supposedly shows superior virtue. Perhaps the worst example is Woodbury's sentimental reaction to the baby at the end of the book: "He knelt beside the cradle, and bent over the sleeping babe, giving way, undisturbed by a watching eye, to the blissful pride of a father's heart. Presently his eyes overflowed with happy tears, and he whispered to the unconscious child: 'Richard! my son, my darling!... God make me worthy to possess thee!'" (461).

Hannah Thurston really has the substance of "soap opera" and of a long string of Hollywood movies of the 1930's. For in both the book and in such movies, woman errs in thinking of freedom as the right to do what men do; she becomes free only as she understands her difference from men and emphasizes that difference. Woman is more idealistic, perceptive, emotional, sympathetic, abstract, moral, conventional; such persons must be shielded from the ugly realities. In return, she furnishes inspiration and shining ideals both to her husband and family and to society.

Still, *Hannah Thurston* is not a bad novel; despite the views of Taylor's other critics, it is his best, chiefly because of the character herself. But there are other good things in the book; for instance, something of the life in a small town is successfully conveyed. Though the emphasis of the satire is women's rights, with lesser attention to Spiritualism and temperance, there are amusing and fairly well-done bits on all the lunacies current at that time—Abolitionism, missionaries, Barnburners, Hunkers, Grahamites, Bethesdaeans, and others. Taylor was, after all, a sophisticated man; and he found the reform fever in America somewhat puzzling and not a little amusing.

II John Godfrey's Fortunes: Related by Himself (*1864*)

Taylor—flushed with the success of *Hannah Thurston* and hopeful that he had at last found a profitable outlet—began *John Godfrey's Fortunes* in March, 1864. This partly satirical novel is the story of the education of a young man and of his winning through to an understanding of the world and himself. Taylor used for the first and only time the first-person narrator, and perhaps for that reason the novel is vaguely reminiscent of *David Copperfield* which had been published in 1850. Taylor said that both *Godfrey* and his third novel, *The Story of Kennett* had been conceived before the first one, but he wrote *Hannah Thurston* first because he did not want to venture his ideas for the other books upon "an experiment." He seems to mean that *Hannah* was an easier idea for a first novel. At any rate, Taylor said little about most of his books after they were finished; he was convinced that he was constantly growing as an author, and for him his best book was always the one he was working on at the time. Thus, he remarked that *Godfrey* was a "much better literary performance" than *Hannah,* that it was "greatly superior . . . in execution," and that it also had had a great sale.[9]

In Taylor's second novel, John Godfrey lives with his widowed mother in Cross Keys, Pennsylvania. She has scrimped to send him to Dr. Dymond's school; John is a good student, and he thinks he may become a writer. When his mother becomes fatally ill, she sends him (and a small legacy) to an uncle who owns a grocery store in Reading. Uncle Wooley, a money-grubbing religious fundamentalist, not only puts him to work but also tries to convert him. As soon as John is old enough, he decides to seek his fortune elsewhere.

After a year of teaching, he decides he wants a literary career; his poetic taste is sentimental, but he has fallen in love with a local girl, Amanda, who agrees to a secret engagement. In New York, he quickly finds that no market exists for poetry, and he gets a job "condensing the miscellaneous" for the *Daily Wonder* at six dollars a week. After a year he decides to publish his own poems; and, with a fancy, leather-bound copy, he returns to Amanda, only to find she has just married his *bête noire,* Charley Rand. He also finds that his uncle has invested and, he fears, lost his legacy in a speculation. Returned to New York, Godfrey is soon promoted to reporter at fifteen dollars a week; and he falls under the baneful influence of Arthur Brandagee, an irreverent, pretentious writer *manqué.* When Godfrey attends literary soirées, he meets such luminaries as Adeliza Choate; and also he meets and likes wealthy Isabel Haworth.

Disillusioned at the falsity of women and with the world because of his loss of Amanda, Godfrey indulges in a Byronic misanthropy; with Brandagee and other habituées of "The Cave," a bar, he helps plan a literary scandal magazine, *The Oracle.* One evening he is sent to report a fire in a house of prostitution, during the course of which he helps one of the inmates to escape. Later, he finds her a job; and one night he meets her in Washington Square to hear her "story." When he later visits Isabel Haworth, he is dismissed without explanation. With this blow, he becomes totally cynical; he spends more and more time drinking in The Cave, quits his job, runs into debt, moves to a cheap room, and lets his clothes become shabby. *The Oracle,* his only source of income, fails; and he finally sinks to writing jingles for toothpaste. When he discovers that Brandagee has even been cheating him of some toothpaste money, he staggers out of the bar into the arms of Bob Simmons, a boyhood chum, who takes him home, sobers him, and helps him begin the long climb back. Bob Simmons is the long-lost love of Jane Berry, the prostitute; and Godfrey is forced to tell him the truth about her. Bob is mortified; Jane decides she isn't worthy to marry him; and their relationship is left ambiguous.

Bob, who is honest and simple, reinspires Godfrey with the goodness of humanity. Godfrey gets his job back, and he soon receives an apologetic note from Isabel; she explains that she had heard evil gossip about him and had seen him with Jane Berry, the prostitute, in Washington Square. They are soon engaged, although Godfrey worries about the inequality of their fortunes. When Isabel is revealed to be not so rich as rumored, Godfrey is inspired with new vigor. He soon hears that Uncle Wooley's speculation was successful and that Godfrey will himself get twenty thousand dollars. He quits his job to live on his income; quits poetry; and he and Isabel are married. In a closing scene of domestic bliss, Isabel suggests he write a book about his adventures.

This summary cannot begin to convey the complexity of plot, nor the series of fantastic coincidences that help develop it. Aside from these problems, however, the novel is obviously a fragment of autobiography; for it follows closely Taylor's own career—the small town, the boarding school, the brief teaching stint, the poems sent to Philadelphia newspapers, the trip to New York to seek his literary fortune, and so on. Despite Taylor's hatred of biographical identification in books, Albert Smyth, who thought it highly autobiographical, proceeded to identify many of the characters in the New York scenes.[10]

Still, the satire is not bad; and the picture of New York literary life in the 1850's has much validity. The portrayal clearly suggests the difficulties American writers had at that time in simply being honest, in finding publishers, and in making a living. Taylor depicts a world in which advertisers expect a *quid pro quo*, reviewers lambaste new authors or give favorable reviews for a consideration, and new journals hope to succeed through a kind of blackmail—as for example, Brandagee's version of how *The Oracle* will succeed: "Once let *The Oracle* become *the* oracle of opinion . . . and you see what our recommendation will be worth. Why, two or three theatres alone would club together to keep up a paper which sent the public to their ticket-offices. . . . We have a positive power, and the exercise of power is just what commands the highest price . . ." (396-97).

Taylor's satires of the literary world are quite funny; in this one, Adeliza Choate explains how she writes:

> . . . I feel the approach of Inspiration in every nerve. . . . It always comes on about three o'clock in the afternoon when the wind blows from the south. I change my dress, and put on a long white gown, which I wear at no other time, take off my stays, and let my hair down my back. Then I prance up and down the room as if I was possessed, and as the lines come to me I *dash* them on the blackboard, one after another, and chant them in a loud voice. Sometimes I cover all four of the boards—both sides—before the Inspiration leaves me. The frail Body is overcome by the excitement of the Soul, and at night my husband often finds me lying on the floor in the middle of the room, panting . . panting! (275)

Taylor also portrays a Walt Whitman-like poet who keeps saying: "Life's the thing! A strong-backed 'long-shore-man, with his hairy and sunburnt arms, and the tobacco-juice in the corners of his mouth, is worth all your saints!" (278).

The satire is neither sharp nor mean-spirited, for the conditions of Taylor's existence in such a world made it impossible for him to be really critical of anyone in public. When he was serious, though, he could also be perceptive, as the following passage demonstrates:

> The fact is, we had no criticism, worthy of the name, at that time. Our literature was tenderly petted, and its diffuse, superficial sentiment was perhaps even more admired than its first attempts at a profounder study of its own appropriate themes and a noble assertion of its autonomy. . . . All our gentle, languishing echoes found spellbound listeners, whom no one—with perhaps, the single exception of Poe—had the will to disenchant. Hillhouse and Dawes, Grenville Mellen and Brainard still sat high on Parnassus, and Griswold astonished us by disinterring a whole Pantheon of forgotten worthies. (227-28)

Taylor has been praised for his use of local color in these novels. It is not bad, particularly in *The Story of Kennett;* but

it should be pointed out how feeble his dialect is—all too often
it is merely ungrammatical speech. For instance, Godfrey's friend,
Bob Simmons, talks like this: "You can write a'most like copy-
plate, and I make the roughest kind o' pot-hooks. The bones o'
your fingers is no thicker than a girl's. I dunno what I'd do if
mine was like that." If the elisions were written out here, the
dialect would consist entirely of two grammatical errors.

Taylor's mild anti-Semitism appears in this novel in an ag-
gressive, risqué character named Miss Levi. The villain's well-
deserved punishment is to marry her and have his house "fre-
quented by numbers of persons with large noses and narrow
stripes of forehead." A similar attitude prevails about the Irish;
when Godfrey visits Mary Maloney, he notices "a very disagree-
able smell . . . which may be found wherever the poor Irish con-
gregate." The central thesis of the book, however, does not lie
in such prejudices, nor in the satire, but in John Godfrey's history. The boy grows into manhood, tries to expand his experience, is disappointed and disillusioned, sinks to the depths (as
Taylor conceives them), and finally reasserts his faith in men and
in life itself.

The major weakness of the novel is, however, that the regeneration is not believable. Godfrey is disillusioned by the malice,
dishonesty, and fraudulence he encounters—in his Uncle Wooley,
who used his money; in Amanda, for whom out of sight is out
of mind; in the literary world, which consists of fakers and fifth-
rate hacks. The agent of his regeneration is Bob Simmons, who
represents simplicity, masculine values, and all those qualities
associated with the soil (though he is a bricklayer). The second
agent is, of course, Isabel Haworth, who is almost totally unreal
but is a typical Genteel female: lovely, ethereal, rigidly pure, and
wealthy. One wonders what Godfrey finds of worth in her; she
has neither the intellect, the conscience, nor the sensitivity of
Hannah Thurston. Isabel is simply Genteel.

Through the character of Isabel, however, the book is saying
something different from what Taylor thought he was saying:
success in American life at this time does not consist in intellectual or artistic development, which is neither welcomed nor
encouraged; it consists in accepting the values of the Genteel
world. Despite the evidence of the senses, one must believe in
the goodness of people, in the reality of a Power that makes all

come right in the end, and in the values of purity, simplicity, goodness. Above all, one must find a Genteel female who will steer one right—right into a conventional marriage full of comfort, decency, children, and happiness. One's reward for such a life is quite tangible; Miss Haworth, after all, possesses eighty thousand dollars; but, so he won't feel too bad, Godfrey is allowed twenty thousand dollars of his own, which he has done nothing to earn. This life is the best kind, the story seems to say —the solid, Genteel, middle-class life. This message argues a simple-minded faith in the way things are; but whether this faith is Taylor's, or whether he believed it his audience's, is not easy to tell.

The attitude toward sex, one of the touchstones of gentility, is also perfectly conventional. It is seen as largely the activity of low-class people—Jane Berry's corruption is of this nature, even though she was enticed into prostitution. Godfrey is not even certain that her crime is forgivable: "Whether the folly of a day is to be the misery of a life, or, on the other hand a too easy rehabilitation of woman's priceless purity shall be allowed to lessen the honor of the sex, are the questions which my poor friends were called upon to solve" (510). Godfrey never has any passionate emotions in the company of Isabel Haworth; he feels only the most profound respect. Even in the depths of his degradation, the worst he ever does is get drunk.

John Godfrey's Fortunes is of interest to today's reader because of the view it gives of New York literary life in the 1850's; but, as a novel which gives some insight into either life or experience, it fails. The experience it deals with is not genuine or true to life; it has little originality of perception or feeling. Its viewpoint and the values it proposes are completely conventional. John Godfrey does not achieve success or self-knowledge, but respectability—the great ideal of the Genteel tradition.

III   The Story of Kennett (*1866*)

Taylor's third novel, *The Story of Kennett*, was finished in January and published in April, 1866. Widely admired, it was revived as late as 1933 as a pageant in Kennett Square, where it was, we are assured, extremely well received. Taylor's two previous novels had created some reputation, for some six thousand copies of Kennett were ordered in advance of publication. The book "was received, not only by a larger public, but also by a more unanimous press. The idyllic character of the work, its freedom from burning questions, and its objectivity gave it great popularity," said his wife.[11]

Taylor, as usual, jubilantly quoted his colleagues: Whittier, for example, said the novel contained "as good things as there are in the English language";[12] Howells wrote that it was "the best historical (historical in the sense of retrospective) novel ever written in America."[13] And later critics have also said good things about it. For Smyth, it was Taylor's best novel, "a true idyll of Pennsylvania country life."[14] Even Beatty thought it had a freshness, simplicity, and freedom from weak satire which made it the most readable of the novels. He praised it especially for local-color characters, and for depictions of barn-raisings and corn-huskings.[15]

Certainly Taylor himself took his novel seriously. "It is totally different from the others,—altogether objective in subject and treatment," he said; and, while he usually thought his current work his best, the following statement to Longfellow is pretty strong: "I have worked earnestly and faithfully during the past three or four years, and finally come to look upon the ventures of this year (my "Story of Kennett" and "Picture of St. John") as being destined to decide the question whether I was to have any place in our literature...."[16] It is melancholy to think that, if Taylor had really rested his case on these two works, he would have lost.

The "objectivity" Taylor mentions seems puzzling, but he probably means that the novel, being set in the eighteenth century, did not depend on his personal experience for its characters and incidents. His wife asserted that the novel possessed "intenser action" and "more imaginative form" than his previous novels, and that "in this work he raised a monument, as it were, to the neighbourhood of his birth. Truth and fiction were woven into its tissue; descriptions of the idyllic scenery in the midst of which he was born, delineations of typical characters among the old Quaker families, and the traditions of a bold highwayman whom his father remembered, are interwoven with the fortunes of the hero."[17] He dedicated the book to his neighbors in Kennett Square, and he clearly had some idea of commemorating his youth in the area where he had grown up. Certainly, "idyllic" is one of the words most used to describe the book. As Taylor remarked in his preface: "In these days, when Fiction prefers to deal with abnormal characters and psychological problems more or less exceptional or morbid, the attempt to represent the elements of life in a simple, healthy, pastoral community, has been to me a source of uninterrupted enjoyment."

The opening scene of the novel occurs before the local tavern, where a group of fox hunters gathers; at their head is Alf Barton, in his late forties, a boastful, cowardly son of a miserly land-owner. The appearance of Gilbert Potter causes grumbling be-cause he has the best horse and because he is "base-born." Gilbert is sensitive about his heritage, for he is hard-working, dependable, and courageous; but his mother tells him only that she was legally wed and that she will reveal the truth about his father at the proper time.

Gilbert wins the chase and gives the fox tail to Martha Deane, the virtuous heiress of Dr. Deane, a wealthy Quaker physician; Gilbert secretly loves Martha. Her father objects to Gilbert and advocates Alf Barton as suitor; he and Old Man Barton, the father of Alf, agree for financial reasons to sponsor the marriage of their children. Alf, however, feels the superiority of Martha; and he is relieved when she rejects him. Later, Gilbert and Martha confess their love but agree to keep it secret until Gil-bert has paid the mortgage on his house and can be financially independent.

During the fox hunt, Alf was robbed by Sandy Flash, a notor-ious highwayman. Later, Flash boldly appears in town, cowing everyone except Gilbert. Flash mysteriously says that Gilbert need not fear him, a remark that worries Gilbert, who thinks Flash may be his father. Later, on his way to Chester with the mortgage money, Gilbert is robbed by Flash, who thinks the money belongs to Barton. On the way home, Gilbert is caught in a flood and nearly drowned; but he is saved by Roger, his intelligent horse, who goes for help.

Gilbert has befriended Deb Smith, an ugly, hard-drinking woman who works around the neighborhood; she, it turns out, is Sandy Flash's mistress. She promises Gilbert he will get his money back; but, when she cannot persuade Flash to return it, she, in rage, betrays him and offers the reward money to

Gilbert. Sandy is sentenced to hang; but, before he dies, he tells Gilbert where the money is and assures him he is not his father.

The answer to the mystery of Gilbert's paternity is eventually revealed when Old Man Barton dies and when, in one of the most repulsive scenes in literature, Gilbert's mother, asking her son to obey without question, visits the corpse. This sentimental scene reveals that Old Man Barton was her father-in-law, that she has been married for twenty-six years to Alf, and that Gilbert is Alf's son. She has suffered in silence because Alf swore her to secrecy for fear of losing his inheritance. But Old Man Barton knew the truth, having been informed by Betsy Lavender; she had guessed it by noticing the similarity between Gilbert's shoulders and Alf's. In the will, Mary Potter (now Barton) gets twenty thousand dollars; Gilbert, five thousand dollars; Alf gets only the farm which will revert to Gilbert—who finds it hard to say "Dad" to the villain of the novel. Dr. Deane now allows Gilbert to marry his daughter. Quivering and despicable Alf, the remaining problem, is sternly forgiven by Mary Barton; perhaps they will live together again.

This plot must seem absurd to any reader; but it does not seem quite so bad while one is reading since the characters, the local color, and other qualities have some interest. Some of the absurdity lies in the details; some, in the handling. For instance, the whole plot depends on the mystery of Gilbert's birth; but it is hard for a modern reader to accept the importance of being "base-born," though it is supposedly the eighteenth century; and having the hero saved from drowning by an intelligent horse more than strains credulity. But the crucial identification made by Betsy—that Alf and Gilbert are related—by noting the shape of their shoulders is simply preposterous. These flaws would be serious in any book; for plot, after all, must have some relation to a probable reality.

The two central scenes in the book have occasioned much comment. The long drawn-out climax at the funeral—when Gilbert's mother insists on her pound of flesh—has occasioned nearly universal repulsion; and it is hard to imagine what possessed Taylor to write the scene. It argues some defect in his view of things—some irrational dedication to the abstraction of honor; for it presents Mary Potter as a vindictive and merciless woman.

Her feeling may be understandable, but it diminishes her stature. Even Smyth thought the scene "a repulsive one, and the reader recoils from its horror and shame."[18] Taylor's contemporaries also objected to it; and his wife admitted that, among the chorus of praise, it was the "only one passage [which] received condemnation."

But Taylor defended it as "the most powerful, most dramatic, most (by all the principles of art and life) justifiable chapter in the book." His defense is based on logic, but it lacks common sense: "Whatever the acknowledged relationship might be to him, to her it was honor—yea, more than honor; for by so much and so cruelly as she had fallen below the rights of her pure name as a woman, the higher would she now be set, not only in respect, but in the reverence earned by her saintly patience and self-denial" (409). However, the scene is still melodramatic, still unprepared for, and still not in keeping with the characters in the rest of the book.

The other important scene, but one much admired, is the betrothal in the woods. Smyth called it "the most exquisite incident of the kind in American literature," an opinion in which many other critics have concurred. It is somewhat painful, therefore, to have to say that this scene is also dreadful, though in a different way from the other one. However, by perusing the kernel of the scene quoted below, the reader may judge for himself. Gilbert loves Martha silently, for she is socially superior. They are riding one day when her saddle girth breaks; Gilbert helps her dismount:

She bent forward and laid her hands upon his shoulders. Then, as she slid gently down, his right arm crept around her waist, holding her so firmly and securely that she had left the saddle and hung in its support while her feet had not yet touched the earth. Her warm breath was on Gilbert's forehead; her bosom swept his breast, and the arm that until then had supported, now swiftly, tenderly irresistibly embraced her. Trembling, thrilling from head to foot, utterly unable to control the mad impulse of the moment, he drew her to his heart and laid his lips to hers. All that he would have said—all, and more than all, that words could have expressed—was now said, without words. His kiss clung as if it were the last this side of death—clung until he felt that Martha feebly strove to be released.

The next minute they stood side by side, and Gilbert, by a
revulsion equally swift and overpowering, burst into a passion of tears.

He turned and leaned his head against Roger's neck. Presently
a light touch came upon his shoulder.

"Gilbert!"

He faced her then, and saw that her own cheeks were wet.
"Martha," he cried, "unless you love me with a love like mine for
you, you can never forgive me!"

She came nearer; she laid her arms around him, and lifted her
face to his. Then she said, in a tender, tremulous whisper:

"Gilbert—Gilbert! I forgive you."

A pang of wonderful, incredulous joy shot through his heart.
Exalted by his emotion above the constraints of his past and present
life, he arose and stood free and strong in his full stature as a man.
He held her softly and tenderly embraced, and a purer bliss than
the physical delight of her warm, caressing presence shone upon
his face as he asked:

"Forever, Martha?"

"Forever." (140-42)

Of its kind, this scene is well done, and may still be moving
to some readers; but it is thoroughly Genteel. The kiss is all right,
but the reactions of Gilbert are certainly odd. In this as in all
of Taylor's love scenes, one may see a certain conception of the
relationship between the sexes; the key word is "purity." Gilbert
bursts into tears, is ashamed of his passion, and considers the
kiss a violation of Martha's purity. The elements of this concept
are that women are pure; men, coarse and rough; and love, an
elevating sentiment rather than a passion, is to be practiced only
with lower-class women or after the legal forms have been
observed. Taylor is fond of such words as "sacred," "hallowed,"
"pure," and "holy" when he talks of love; and he appears to
mean them.

But *Kennett* has other qualities. The eighteenth-century setting does not seem to have much point, except that it allows
use of the legend of Sandy Flash and that it also gives some
objective distance to the whole narrative. The details of country
life, such as the barn-raising, do have some historical interest.
And, in a way, the minor characters like Deb Smith and Betsy
Lavender are more attractive and believable than the major ones.
The major characters embody a sort of official point of view that
Taylor feels he must support—gentlemanly and womanly qual-

ities, ideals of dignity and honor—but the minor people can be more realistic, colloquial, and vulgar.

As might be expected from an old farm boy, Taylor's knowledge of country life is also impressive. He knows external nature well—the names of flowers, trees, and living creatures; and his descriptions of these things are well-done: "The country was now covered with the first fresh magnificence of summer. The snowy pyramids of dogwood bloom had faded, but the tulip trees were tall cones of rustling green, lighted with millions of orange-colored stars, and all the underwood beneath the hemlock forests by the courses of streams, was rosy with laurels and azaleas . . ." (102). In an age that put a premium on descriptive writing, Taylor had pretty well mastered it.

Quakerism, a recurrent minor theme in these novels, is presented as a repressive force whose virtues must also be respected. A pervasive influence in the rural life, it is characterized by the suppression of feeling and by the emotional impoverishment of its adherents. Of a speaker at a Quaker meeting, Taylor says: "A close connection of ideas, a logical derivation of argument from text, would have aroused their suspicions that the speaker depended rather upon his own active, conscious intellect than upon the moving of the spirit; but this aimless wandering of a half-awake soul through the cadences of a language which was neither song nor speech was, to their minds, the evidence of genuine inspiration" (79). Taylor was not a Quaker, but, since the influence of Quakerism was strong where he grew up, he was quite familiar with the principles of the sect.

The other side of Taylor's concern with repressiveness is the desire his characters often express for more open expression of feeling, especially between men. In this novel, as in his others, he depicts a close friendship between two men; but, when Gabriel is moved to embrace his friend, he stops suddenly: "It was not the custom of the neighborhood; the noblest masculine friendship would have been described by the people in no other terms than 'They are very thick,' and men who loved each other were accustomed to be satisfied with the knowledge" (237). This theme is explored more extensively in his last novel, *Joseph and His Friend*.

A sturdy bourgeois sense of financial responsibility is also one of the cornerstones of this book. Gilbert works hard to pay off his mortgage; and, when he is robbed, it is like the end of the world. "His indebtedness," commented Taylor, "carried with it a sense of stern and perpetual responsibility, which, alas, has not always been inherited by the descendants of that simple and primitive period" (221). And virtue is rewarded, as in the other novels, very concretely; Gilbert at the end of the novel enjoys considerable wealth and comfort.

Generally, one finds it difficult to agree with critical opinions that regard *The Story of Kennett* as Taylor's best novel. The love affair is highly genteel, the mystery of Gilbert's birth is ridiculous, the local legends about Sandy Flash are interesting but not significant, and the plotting is loose and sometimes strained. The chief interest lies in minor characters and in the picture of rural life in Pennsylvania. Throughout the novel, one finds Taylor's ambiguous attitudes toward the country. He likes simplicity, plain virtues, nature, landscape, and, when he can sentimentalize them, even the people. On the other hand, he knows from experience how smothering and repressive rural life is—how stunting to the sensitive and intelligent—and he hates that aspect of it.

IV Joseph and His Friend (*1870*)

Taylor's last novel, *Joseph and His Friend,* was begun in January, 1869, and published in November, 1870; the only one serialized before publication, it first appeared in *The Atlantic Monthly.* Since it was published at the same time as Part I of *Faust,* the novel did not receive much attention from the public. Taylor had not had the time to concentrate on this novel because of his attention to *Faust*; nonetheless, he considered it "my best novel, with all its deficiencies."

Actually his least successful and most intensely disliked novel, the reaction to *Joseph and His Friend* may have helped persuade Taylor to stop writing novels. Smyth, for example, found it repulsive and dismissed it with this remark: "It is an unpleasant story of mean duplicity and painful mistakes. The characters are shallow and their surroundings mean. There is not a single pleasing situation or incident in the book."[19] Taylor's own statement of his intentions was a bit cryptic: "... what I attempted to do was to throw some indirect light on the great questions which underlie civilized life, and the existence of which is only dimly felt, not intelligently perceived, by most Americans. I allowed the plot to be directed by these *cryptic* forces; hence, a reader who does not feel them will hardly be interested in the external movement of the story."[20] He admitted, however, that "the blessed half-educated public sees nothing in the book but dulness." These "great questions" and "cryptic forces" were never defined. But the evasiveness of the statement, as well as the book itself, seems to support the thesis that Taylor was talking about sexual problems.

Joseph, an orphaned, shy, immature twenty-two, lives with his religious Aunt Rachel on a large farm in Pennsylvania. He goes to a party for a city visitor, Julia Blessing, whose artful charm pleases everyone. Although Joseph was interested in Lucy Henderson, he is now drawn to Julia Blessing; and, when she hears of his valuable farm, she becomes interested in him. Elwood Withers, the hearty masculine friend of Joseph, proposes to Lucy but is rejected. Both Withers and Lucy worry about Joseph's infatuation with Julia, but he has already committed himself by this time to marry her.

Soon Joseph visits Julia's family in Philadelphia. The Blessings are shabby-genteel; the father is a small-time politician, a Dickensian character who accepts his future son-in-law immediately when he learns Joseph's farm is worth twenty-six thousand dollars. Accidentally, Joseph learns that Julia is actually thirty years old. On the train home, he meets the "friend" of the title, a worldly, sympathetic man of twenty-eight named Philip Held; and their meeting is described as if theirs was a love affair. He is on the way to Joseph's area to manage a forge, and he reveals that he was once interested in Julia's sister.

Joseph and Julia are married; he asks her for perfect openness and sympathy; but he soon finds her shallow and artful. She makes costly changes around the farm, criticizes his friends, and aspires to give social law to the neighborhood. Her father borrows money and induces Joseph to invest in oil; Aunt Rachel, meanwhile, has packed up and left. Joseph frequently visits Philip and the Hopetons, Philip's friends. There is gradually revealed a tangled skein of frustrated loves: Joseph dislikes his wife; Lucy loves Joseph; Elwood, Lucy; Philip, Mrs. Hopeton.

Joseph gets frequent requests for more money on the investment, and he gives Mr. Blessing his power of attorney to sell the shares. When Joseph later visits the wells, he is convinced they are a swindle. On a visit to Philip, he is so depressed by his situation that he is tempted to jump off a cliff, but Philip stops him. Philip then confesses his love for Mrs. Hopeton and proposes that he and Joseph run away together and start over again elsewhere.

Julia, who turns out to be a diabolical schemer, asks Lucy to help her win Joseph's love. When Lucy tries to talk with Joseph in the garden, he confesses that he hates Julia; and, at that moment, Julia bursts out of the bushes, accuses them of making love, and threatens to blackmail them. She then runs into the house, reappears soon after in a disheveled condition, accuses him of killing her, and falls dead.

When town gossip holds that Joseph killed her, he demands an investigation, and his friends work to prove his innocence. At the trial, evidence favors the prosecution; but, at the crucial moment, Philip bursts into court with the proper witness, who proves that Julia bought the arsenic in Lucy's name. Mr. Blessing reveals that Julia used it for her complexion; her death was, therefore, accidental.

Lucy now accepts Elwood's marriage proposal; but Joseph decides to travel to the West and to retrace Philip's steps there in hope of acquiring his maturity. The oil investment has become a success, and Joseph's shares are worth twenty-five thousand dollars. Finally, it is suggested that Joseph and his friend's sister may later be married.

As is evident, this book is not much different from the other novels. It has most of Taylor's stock characters: for example, the fatherless boy living with an older woman, usually his mother but here an aunt, who is usually a Quaker. (In *Hannah Thurston*, the female character lives alone with a Quaker mother.) There is the hearty masculine friend who appears in all the books, in this case not Philip but Elwood; he functions as an exemplar to the main character of uncomplicated and direct action, especially with women. There is the usual pair of women, good and bad; there is the usual rescue from drowning (a symbol of courage to Taylor); and there is the seemingly lost investment which turns out well, leaving the hero rich as the tale ends. Moreover, the setting in all four books begins, at least, in a small farming community.

But *Joseph and His Friend* has unusual features; indeed it is not his best novel, but it is certainly his most peculiar. The relationship between its male characters would be enough to assure its oddity in 1869. The first oddity is that the book is about a bad marriage, for Taylor's other novels end with marriage and happiness; this one begins with marriage and shows its collapse; and it ends with the hero happier as a widower. In *John Godfrey*, the hero finds out painfully what is it to love the wrong woman and to lose her; but he finally makes the right choice. Joseph's story concerns, however, the miseries of the wrong choice; and the assumption, of course, is that nothing can be done about such a decision, for divorce is not even mentioned.

The portrait of Julia, while somewhat overdrawn, is an effective picture of the selfish, self-centered woman who is deceitful, secretive, and spoiled. Her character is unusually nasty for Taylor; indeed, she is his only really repulsive character. But her portrayal is too exaggerated; her blackmail attempt is absurd; and the suggestion that she killed herself to frame Joseph is unfair to the reader. The death scene is unusually dreary; and the account of the investigation, as well as the courtroom scene at the end, threatens at times to turn the book into a mystery novel.

Nonetheless, the suggestions of homosexuality in the book can hardly be overlooked. Certainly, the relationship between Joseph and his friend has such overtones. Scenes of their embracing and kissing each other make the reader somewhat uncomfortable. Yet it is by no means certain that the book should be interpreted this way.

Still, there are many odd passages in this book. After Philip prevented Joseph's suicide, "he led him to the bank, sat down beside him, and laid his arm about his neck. The silence and the caress were more soothing to Joseph than any words" (171). In another scene, "their hands closed upon each other, and they were entirely happy in the tender and perfect manly love which united them" (340). One of the climactic scenes reads: "They took each other's hands. The day was fading, the landscape was silent, and only the twitter of nesting birds was heard in the boughs above them. Each gave way to the impulse of his manly love, rarer, alas! but as tender and true as the love of woman, and they drew nearer and kissed each other. As they walked back and parted on the highway, each felt that life was not wholly unkind, and that happiness was not yet impossible" (217).

The emphasis on "manly" love suggests Whitman, and perhaps Taylor derived the idea, or the encouragement to write about it, from Whitman, to whom there are many references in his books, though most are unfavorable. It is interesting to note that Whitman, like Taylor, had a Quaker background; for the repressions of Quakerism probably had something to do with this question. Taylor evidently felt that Quakerism led to the stigmatizing of feelings with which there was nothing wrong; and Quakerism was one of the things from which he was escaping. *Joseph and His Friend* may be Taylor's outcry against this repression. "Why do men so carefully conceal what is deepest and strongest in their natures?" asks Joseph. And elsewhere, Philip says to him: "A man's perfect friendship is rarer than a woman's love, and most hearts are content with one or the other . . ." (112).

Taylor had many close relationships with men (Bufleb springs immediately to mind); and the type of relationship that is depicted in the novel was more normal in the nineteenth century than today. Male friendships were closer and more casual because relationships with women were more formal and artificial. Benjamin Franklin could offer health as a reason for practicing "venery," but a man of Taylor's time could not openly offer that or any other excuse; for attitudes toward marriage, women, and family life forbade it.

The changes in sex attitudes that have occurred can only be characterized as improvements; but these changes have been enormous—if one judges them on the basis of the contrast between twentieth- and nineteenth-century fiction. If the love affairs in Taylor's novels have any relation at all to truth, then satisfactory relationships with "decent" women were next to impossible. Indeed, a prominent feature of the Genteel tradition was the presentation of such relationships in the most unreal terms possible. Perhaps Taylor was presenting an adverse view of this very situation. He was, after all, a traveled and sophisticated man who had seen things he didn't write about; he had been where the culture of the Anglo-Saxons hadn't penetrated and where older, more natural attitudes prevailed. Certainly one finds suggestions of his interest in other views in his books about Africa and his affection for the Arabs. It is hard to believe, therefore, that he seriously held the Genteel values reflected in these novels. Yet, aside from scandalizing his neighbors by importing liquor and tobacco, his activities and views seem for the most part conventional. He was certainly not a radical on any subject.

Whatever Taylor's motive, the book is somewhat confused. But one thing is clear: although the story has much of the usual relationships between men and women, its real center is that between the two men. Friendship and love are, after all, different degrees of the same feeling, not different feelings. In the 1970's, such a theme would hardly excite notice, but for 1869 it seems daring.

V. Beauty and the Beast: and Tales of Home (*1872*)

From time to time, Taylor also wrote short stories, perhaps a dozen or so; since no bibliography exists of his journal contributions, it is difficult to know exactly how many. Most were published during the 1860's in *The Atlantic Monthly* while it was edited by his friend and publisher, James T. Fields. In 1872 Taylor collected his stories for a volume, *Beauty and the Beast,* containing eight stories and a novella; he had previously added two stories to fill out the volume *At Home and Abroad* (Second Series). These eleven pieces give a good idea of his work in this genre.

The stories are not much different from the novels in material, attitudes, and quality. The same themes recur: satirical attacks on reformers, on women's rights, and on Spiritualism. There are two Quaker stories, and other accounts of country life that have a love interest. Two are mysteries, and the last, "Beauty and the Beast," is a Russian tale Taylor had heard on his journeys. Nearly all, with the exception of the satirical stories, contain a Genteel love story which is the real center of interest.

Among the tales that deal with country life, "Twin-Love" is certainly the most peculiar; and what readers of the *Atlantic* made of it can only be conjectured. The narrative concerns twin brothers, Jonathan and David, between whom exist sympathies of an unusual nature—they become ill if parted, can sense what each other is thinking, and spend much time fondling and kissing each other. When their mother dies, they are fourteen, and their father encourages separation; he suggests they might someday want to marry women, an idea that hadn't occurred to them. But they promise to try living apart, and one of them becomes interested in a girl, Ruth. The idea of permanent separation frightens them, but they are reconciled to the idea, especially after Ruth kisses the wrong brother.

When Jonathan marries Ruth, David goes west; but he still communes with his brother occasionally near a great ash tree. Years pass; Ruth has three children, then falls ill; and Jonathan in distress calls his brother with his heart (yes, with his heart). David returns, and the twins are happily reunited while they watch Ruth slowly die. The odd callousness of the brothers toward Ruth is overshadowed by the odder relationship between the brothers. The story shows something of Taylor's belief in occult powers; and its point seems to be that one can't separate identical twins—but that idea is absurd. Rather, it is a trying-out of the material of *Joseph and His Friend,* for it constantly skirts the edge of suggestive sexuality.

The other two country stories depend on far-fetched coincidence and on Genteel love. In "Jacob Flint's Journey," a pathologically shy young man is mocked by the local yokels. When his father discovers his trouble, he gives him money to go away for a month. Outside the community, people treat him normally, and he begins to act more normally; he falls in love with a farmer's daughter. His father agrees to the marriage with one peculiar condition: he must pretend to be a hired man, and she must consent to be his father's housekeeper for a week. When the week is over, her parents appear; and her mother turns out to be an old love of Jacob's father, whom he had wronged years before. Now all is forgiven, the children will get the farm, and all is happy.

The idea that others accord one the respect one demands has some validity, but Taylor spoils his story with an overcomplicated plot. Of course, he has to fulfill the "journey" of the title, but for the girl's mother to be an ex-friend of Jacob's father is, in story terms, pointless, as is the father's pretense that Jacob is a hired hand. The love affair itself is genteel, but it is too sketchy to be as clearly bad as some of the others that Taylor concocted.

"Miss Bartram's Trouble" is, however, hopelessly genteel. A city girl, Emily Bartram, is attracted while visiting a friend's farm to an adopted son, Leonard Clare, a rough, masculine, diamond—crude, vulgar, and untutored. As a sign of love, she begins to correct his grammar; but her problem is whether or not the labor of turning him into a gentleman is worth the work; she finally decides it is a major project and declines. Years later, when she marries, another wedding takes place across the street; and she faints when she sees the groom who, one presumes, is Clare. Ten years later, widowed, she is on a steamship which catches fire. Instantly, a handsome, cultured man puts her into his raft; he is Clare who, with her early inspiration, made himself into a gentleman—he has even kept a pressed flower which she had given him years before. Naturally, he is a widower; and, when they see a sail coming, the reader may easily conjecture the results. The handling of this story is very poor; once again, there is too much plot and too many coincidences.

In "The Strange Friend," a family of unusual Quakers appears in a rural community to rent a farm. Henry Donnelly is Irish, has money, and seems too worldly to the Quakers. He wins the confidence of the community by working hard, paying bills, and speaking at meetings. But the Donnellys are not in fact serious Quakers, but are temporarily in exile. Soon the family retainer appears to tell them that their castle is clear of debt and that they can return to Ireland. It is not easy to say whether the curious callousness shown here is Taylor's recognition of a reality, or simply a blind spot in his own perception. The casual way in which Donnelly's deception of his neighbors is dismissed recalls the similar callousness of "Twin-Love." But "The Strange Friend" is hardly a story; it gets nowhere and means nothing.

Taylor has trouble keeping a center to his stories; he is too much tempted to add more plot, more characters, and more love interest. His stories have little unity, and they contain too much irrelevant material; and, though Taylor spoke highly of Poe, Taylor apparently didn't learn much from him about the art of the short story. Some interest is developed here in the scenes of Quaker life, which is presented understandingly and sympathetically. The sect is seen as upright, hard-working, faithful, and, ironically, as interested in wealth, but helpful to their own kind. But Taylor also presents them as unimaginative, rigid, and unintentionally cruel.

Another Quaker story, "Friend Eli's Daughter," begins well as an account of the bias of the sect against marrying outsiders; but it bogs down in overplotting, happy endings, and Genteel piety. Eli Michenor offers his farm as refuge to the weakly son of a friend, despite the fact that he, Richard Hilton, is "one of the world's people." When Richard and Eli's daughter Asenath (she has a "protecting atmosphere of purity and truth") fall in love, her father refuses permission for them to marry and sends Richard away. Later, when Eli and Asenath visit Philadelphia, they meet a drunken bum who is, of course, Richard. He abuses Eli; Asenath, who replies with kind but severe criticism, decides that "It was better to think of him as a purified spirit, waiting to meet her in a holier communion. . . ." Years pass; she never marries; and then a speaker stirs the local meeting with a tale of degeneration and regeneration. He is the reformed Richard, who has taken another name; he and Asenath leave together with father's approval. Once again, the account of Quaker life is good, especially that of the meetings. Eli's rigidity is well portrayed, and Asenath's depiction is reasonably successful. But, while it may be possible that men can be reformed by love for a woman, it happens to more men in Taylor's stories than one can believe possible.

The element of mystery in "The Haunted Shanty" sets it apart from other country stories. Like "The Strange Friend," it lacks a resolution and is hardly in any real sense a story. Its novelty lies in the idea of someone being haunted by a person still alive —in this case, a disappointed fiancée. She had sworn revenge against her old beau; and, after haunting him for years, she can't stop; she has become an instrument of wrath for the punishment of both. However, the haunting exhausts her, and she soon dies. "It was evidently one of those mysterious cases of spiritual disease which completely baffle our reason," said Taylor.

The other mystery, "Can a Life Hide Itself?", a vague Poe-like tale of deduction, is told in the first person by a detective who speculates that "the incredible fatuity of crime" braces one's faith "in the ascendency of Good in the government of the world." A beginning like this one doesn't promise much, and the story doesn't deliver very much. It concerns some scraps of information taken from a derelict and how, from them, the detective deduced marvelous things; but he does so with a good deal of help from Taylor. Later, the narrator checks out his guesses, which prove to be right, to no one's surprise. The official moral is that "Perhaps the surest indication of evil . . . is that it always tries to conceal itself, and the strongest incitement to good is that evil cannot be concealed."

The satirical stories are not of great fictional importance, and they tell little that is new about Taylor's views. "Experiences of the A. C." deals with a group which, under the leadership of a Transcendentalist, agrees to spend the summer living together cleanly and thinking highly. Shelldrake, a pompous, self-deceived man, believes only in "natural" foods; and he easily persuades himself that the food he likes, such as cheese and beer, is natural. The experiment is a failure: some members sneak away to catch fish; others tell the truth only to stir animosities; several refuse to work. Selfishness and egotism are rampant, and the whole colony collapses when Shelldrake, high on beer, flirts with the hero's wife. The author comments: "I see now, more clearly, the causes of these vagaries, which originated in a genuine aspiration, and failed from an ignorance of the true nature of Man." In other words, reformers don't understand human nature. Some scenes are amusing, but the implications of the story point to Taylor's essential conservatism.

Another satirical story, "Mrs. Strongitharm's Report," pretends to be a letter, at some future date, to a newspaper from a leading advocate of women's rights, explaining what happened to the movement. Women wanted, for example, freedom without responsibility; and, when they began to be drafted into the army, they complained bitterly. In the legislature, they quickly began to act like men: they traded votes, were bought by lobbyists, and brawled like others. They were bored by real problems like tariffs, rate reforms, and law-making. The story is ironical since the narrator is unaware of the implications of her words which illustrate that the much-repeated argument of suffragists—that women would bring a higher tone to politics—proves wrong; politics merely corrupts the women. There are some funny bits, and the ironical voice was an unusual feat for Taylor, who didn't try often to achieve such an effect.

"Confessions of a Medium" is the narrative of the experiences of a young man susceptible to "influences." Taylor wanted to keep his authorship of this story a secret, he told Fields, because "I want it to be thought a *bona fide* confession, and was very careful to give it that character. I think it will attract attention."[21] The then editor of the *Atlantic*, Lowell, complimented Taylor on a fine job;[22] and, though it is not clear if the piece excited the reaction Taylor had hoped to attain, the story is well done. The narrator, after describing his experiences, concludes that Spiritualists advocate free expression as a cover for illicit affairs. The condition of the trance "removes the wholesome check which holds our baser passions in subjection." He concludes that Spiritualism is a racket, but he still believes in clairvoyance.

The last story, "Beauty and the Beast," is a novella, the idea for which Taylor, having first heard it during his Russian travels, says he borrowed from a Russian author named Petjerski. It has a very complicated plot, much of which is irrelevant. The town of Kinesma a hundred years ago was ruled by a brutal autocrat named Alexis, whose entertainment consisted in whipping serfs, getting his bear drunk, and giving gigantic hunting parties which culminated in a *reisak,* or having serfs dive through the shallow ice of the Volga River to see if they could come up again. His son, Boris, goes away to St. Petersburg, falls in love with a beautiful and pure female, and marries her. The news infuriates Alexis, who browbeats his own wife to death, then blames his son for her death. Boris brings his wife home, only to find that the people have been instructed to insult them. As their carriage stops at the castle, Alexis flies down the steps with his whip; but, when one glance at the beauty of his daughter-in-law, Helena, paralyzes him, he collapses in a heap. He reforms, gives up drinking, vulgar parties, and beating serfs; but, when her first son dies, he relapses. Helena understands it is "a contest of nature with nature, spiritual with animal power." She provokes him (which isn't hard); he replies in a rage; and he is about to beat her to death with the whip when she begins to sing. Her voice, pure and lovely, paralyzes him again; he again collapses; and his reform this time is permanent. Later she bears Boris a healthy son.

One can't help seeing in this story—as well as in others of

the regeneration of men by women—another more ominous meaning. Animalism, represented by a masculine boor, struggles with the spiritual power, represented by a Genteel female; and the result represents the triumph of spirit over flesh. This concept is essentially, of course, a Christian one; but it could also be read as the triumph of the woman over the man, his ultimate subjection to her whim, and the subjugation of the male to domesticity. The odd effect of this story on a modern male reader is a sneaking admiration for the boor before his transformation. The early Alexis seems more interesting than the transformed one who obediently rocks the baby to sleep on his lap.

A number of Taylor's stories follow this pattern: a man learns that if he wants a paragon of womanhood he must conform to her views and desires; and her desires are for his subjugation, the denial of his masculinity. If one chooses to so interpret these stories they are about the emasculation of American men by the Genteel tradition, which postulates women as morally and spiritually superior and as more deserving of power. Otherwise, this Taylor story is not essentially important. It is too long, complicated, and Genteel; and the idea of a person's being morally regenerated by the mere presence of goodness is trite.

VI *Evaluation of the Fiction*

Plainly, Taylor was not a great writer of fiction—nor even a very good one. With few exceptions, his fiction is dully conventional in technique and material, overplotted, unfocussed, and highly Genteel. Yet, by the standard of his day, when most fiction was Romantic and was written for women readers, his novels are not so bad as the great bulk of fiction; indeed, his are really better than most of it. Nothing of Taylor's is nearly so bad as *Queechy*, or *The Gates Ajar*—both by women, both profoundly sentimental, and both much better sellers than anything Taylor wrote. On the other hand, by the standards of serious literature, Taylor's novels are, by and large, less than mediocre. The most charitable view is simply that fiction was not his métier and that he was a poet—a view he would surely have agreed with.

Still, the question remains as to why a spohisticated and widely read man could produce such weak fiction. Doing so was not unusual; a great deal of Mark Twain's fiction is quite as bad as Taylor's, though nothing of Taylor's is as good as Twain's best. Certainly since Taylor's time there has been a great change in attitudes toward fiction. For one thing, there was then a greater emphasis on the "story" element. Authors did not take the short story seriously; that development came at a later time. Most of Taylor's fiction consists really of "tales"; what interested him was telling a story which seemed interesting, or curious, or odd; but he no doubt often thought they illustrated something important about human nature. He did not probe very deeply into character, nor did he study the ugly side of life. Unlike the Naturalists, he thought that view was not fit material for art. His models were his successful contemporaries in England— Dickens, Thackeray, and Bulwer-Lytton.

The fundamental trouble with Taylor's fiction is that it lacks significance; for a modern reader it has very little usable meaning. One has only to think of another novel of the time, Dostoievsky's *Crime and Punishment*, which was published in the same year as *The Story of Kennett*; but a comparison of the two would be ludicrous. Dostoievsky's probing into the secret recesses of human personality is far beyond anything Taylor ever did or could do; for Dostoievsky was a man of greater perception, understanding, and human compassion. Taylor was not devoid of these qualities, but he lacked depth. It is interesting to note, too, that Dostoievsky was constantly harassed for money; like Taylor, he wrote for money though he lived a much less comfortable life. Yet *Crime and Punishment* is a great book while *The Story of Kennett* is a quaint and dusty romance.

There is room in literature for novels of all sorts and levels; there can be much value in a second- or third-rank novel, as all know who have enjoyed minor classics. There is a place for books like *The Story of Kennett*, and a respectable one; for to write honestly and accurately about an aspect of life in Pennsylvania during a certain epoch is an admirable accomplishment. The truth is simply that books like *Crime and Punishment* furnish one with an idea of the higher limits of the art, and hence the place of such novels as *Kennett* cannot be very high, comparatively speaking.

Taylor's wife made an interesting comment in her memoirs. Speaking of *Hannah Thurston*, from which Taylor read to her

as he wrote, she said: "I could not refrain from playfully chid-
ing him for the realistic delineations that were antagonistic to
my taste—whereupon he only laughed good humouredly. He
very well knew the dualism of his creative faculty and recog-
nised that two different spiritual elements held the balance in his
nature: one idealistic, which constantly urged him to higher
aspiration and showed forth in his poems, the other realistic,
that led him to see life as it actually is."[23]

This passage is revealing, for one notes that "realistic delineations" were antagonistic to her taste. But interesting, too, is the
"dualism" of Taylor, which is not far from the truth. He did
have a strong realistic urge, which found its outlet in the local
color of the stories. In such lesser material as settings and minor
characters, Taylor could indulge his realistic perceptions; but in
the major characters and their genteel love affairs he couldn't be
realistic, for here he expressed his Genteel, or "idealistic," quality that accounts for some aspects of these works and that also
makes them characteristic of his period.

This duality is a major feature of the Genteel Tradition and
of most nineteenth-century fiction, which combines Realism in
the lesser material with an "idealistic" or Romantic quality in the
love relations—these books were intended, after all, for a largely
female audience. This duality helps explain the bewilderment of
a modern reader who admires the local color but is baffled by the
falseness of the characters. It is difficult to say finally whether
such writers were bound by their market or whether they themselves believed in this pervasive unreality.

CHAPTER 4

Poetry

TAYLOR, who wanted to be, above all, a poet, believed he had "the curse,/ Or blessing, which has clung to me from birth—/ The torment and the ecstasy of verse."[1] His other books he considered primarily as money-making activities; indeed, he often remarked that they merely bought time in which to write poetry. Nonetheless, he was engaged in so many ventures— traveling, lecturing, editing, diplomacy—that comparatively little time was left for his verse. He had an excellent memory, and he developed the habit of composing poems in his head so that, when he found time, he could write them down quickly with a minimum of revision. This quality, regarded as a remarkable ability, was, in fact, demanded by practical and financial necessity.

Aside from actually writing poetry, Taylor spent much time developing his poetic reputation. Letters to his friends, which form a constant stream, comment on his latest efforts, ask for praise and reassurance, remark on technical points, explain intentions, and assert confidence that he was growing as a poet. He reminds his friends that he is not really a traveler, lecturer, novelist, diplomat but a poet who has had to spend much time on hack work. His friends—persons much like himself, Boker, Stoddard, Stedman, Aldrich, Fields—usually supplied him with the praise he needed for his work, agreed that he was developing, and shared his contempt for his other activities.

Taylor even extracted praise from the New England Brahmins; Longfellow frequently sent him notes of praise (often in response to a copy of Taylor's latest book), as did Lowell, Whittier, Holmes, and others. Taylor also sedulously cultivated poets and organs of opinion which reviewed books, and he thought there was nothing wrong about doing so; it was simply part of the way one became recognized in America at the time. He often expressed the view that poets should "help" each other—and he meant with praise and favorable reviews. The deference he showed older poets was marked, even approached the disgusting; for he was not above gross flattery. When he was praised, he promptly wrote to his friends, quoting whoever had said his latest book was his best. He had an excessive need of approval and of reassurance that his poetry was as good as he hoped; and his friends quickly realized what was expected.

But, of course, Taylor had enemies. While his publisher, Fields, tried to see that reviews were written by friends, Taylor's work was sometimes reviewed by people who thought his poetry bad. Taylor's publisher, who thought of reviewing as a form of advertising, often either bribed reviewers or wrote reviews himself which he planted anonymously in various journals. The American literary world was such that it is hard to tell if reviewers were critically perceptive, or if they were merely personal or politically enemies (writing for Greeley's *Tribune* automatically made Taylor some enemies). One thing, however, is certain: the reviews are not trustworthy, and it is hard to determine what the real opinion of his verse was.

Taylor sincerely held an exalted idea of the poet and his function. Poetry was, to him, the highest kind of activity. "Born in the purple! born in the purple!/ Heir to the sceptre and crown!"[2] he wrote in one of his poems about poetry. His letters reiterate his conception of the "sacredness" of the poet's office. Essentially, as for many other poets of his era, poetry became for Taylor a substitute for religion. But he began writing poetry under the worst possible auspices—he imitated the magazine and album verse of the day. Sentimental and pious, the verse of such as Mrs. Sigourney, Mrs. Hale, and others of the "gemmiferous" school were his early admirations. To his credit, he outgrew this stage through a combination of wide reading, good advice, and naturally maturing taste.

His first poem, "Soliloquy of a Young Poet," published when he was only sixteen in the *Saturday Evening Post* of Philadelphia, sounded like this:

> High hopes spring up within;
> Hopes of the future—thoughts of glory—fame

Which prompt my mind to toil, and bid me win
That dream—a deathless name.[3]

Other early poems, which are not better, display a handling of
the technical side of verse that is not bad; indeed, technical
variety was always one of his strengths.

Generally, Taylor's early poetry, up to *The Poet's Journal*
(1862) was brief and lyrical; but he became so absorbed in
travel and lecturing that he did not produce a great quantity.
From *Ximena* (1844) to *The Poet's Journal* (1862), a period of
eighteen years, he published only five volumes of verse. With
The Poet's Journal, there came a distinct change in the kind
and quantity. Though he wrote many short lyrics throughout his
life, most subsequent volumes consisted of long narrative or
dramatic poems. *The Poet's Journal* was, therefore, a transitional
work; his first really long poem was *The Picture of St. John*
in 1866. Between this volume and *Prince Deukalion* in 1878,
the year of his death, he published seven volumes of long poems
(not counting *Faust*) and one of shorter pieces.

I   Ximena, or The Battle of the Sierra Morena,
and Other Poems (*1844*)[4]

Taylor's first volume was printed when he was nineteen at his
own expense. He raised the money by subscription among his
neighbors. Fundamentally, of course, he was driven by a powerful ambition, an urge to fame which drove him all his life:
"... I have cherished hopes of occupying at some future day
a respectable station among our country's poets. I believe all
poets are possessed in a greater or less degree of ambition; it
is inseparable from the nature of poetry. And ... I think this
ambition is never given without a mind of sufficient power to
sustain it, and to achieve its lofty object...."[5] As one critic
remarked of the young Taylor, "never did youth entertain fairer
visions of fame than were the possession at this time of this
West Chester lad; never did man have higher and more ab-
stracted ambition; never did a generous and gentle nature pant
more eagerly for recognition and for sympathy."[6]

Taylor's early mentor, sad to report, was none other than
Rufus W. Griswold, the infamous traducer of Poe. A literary

power and the editor of *Graham's Magazine*, Griswold gave Taylor advice and help; and Taylor dedicated his first book to him. But Taylor's attachment to Griswold did not end with this dedication; he introduced Stoddard to him, and they were part of a group that met for many years in the chambers of the good doctor (Griswold), "who enjoyed a doubtful distinction as the chief herdsman of our Parnassian fold."[7]

Ximena contained fifteen poems so forgettable that even their author forgot them; he never reprinted any. They displayed, said a later critic, a "faint lyrical quality," reflections of his readings, and an "affection for Scott, Byron, Moore, and Mrs. Hemans."[8] The breathings of the author's youthful soul were not indicative of unusual promise, said another, though the verse was "sonorous" and showed Taylor's "ambition and facile gift."[9]

The collection includes such poems as "Nature's Inspiration" in Bryant-like blank verse that urges the reader to "commune alone with Nature's majesty,/ And feel the presence of an unseen Power." "The Dream of Fame," also in blank verse, concerns a young man who seeks fame ("Oh, vain and mad presumption!"); but he finds that doing good deeds makes his death sweeter. There are poems to Pennsylvania, to the Brandywine, to the Catskills (where the poet's senses reeled at the sight!). Most are descriptive, and they are full of Popean epithets, personifications, and abstractions. The volume shows metrical skill, but the subjects are conventional. These poems may be the "sincere and fervent effusions of his heart," but there is little that forecasts unusual talent; the poetry is quite commonplace.

II Rhymes of Travel, Ballads and Poems (*1849*)

Taylor's second volume of poetry, *Rhymes of Travel*, was published in December, 1848, two years after his return from his first European tour. It contains forty-four poems, only twenty-four of which have survived in later editions. The volume has the distinction of having been criticized by Edgar Allan Poe, who found "glowing imagination" and "sonorous well-balanced rhythm" in one poem titled "The Continents."[11] But it is not easy to find such qualities now in that poem, a patriotic effusion in which continents are personified.

Stedman, however, thought these poems not remarkable "even as a poet's first offering"; and Taylor was twenty-four years old, hardly a "precocious singer."[12] The truth is that the poems are almost universally bad. About topics like "Freedom," "Life," and "Evil," they are vague, pretentious, abstract, platitudinous, and generally without any significant meaning. Most were written in Europe during Taylor's travels, and they often describe a scene or a monument. Westminster Abbey inspired him to write "The Poet's Ambition":

> But purer, holier, loftier is the aim
> Born of his gift divine;
> His spirit longs to grasp that crown of fame,
> Whose stars forever shine.

None of these verses has any life or reality for a modern reader; they are genteel, imitative, and rhetorical.

The "Picturesque Ballads of California," however, are an oddity; for Taylor wrote them before he had visited the West. They began as a sort of lark, and they were published anonymously in the *Literary World* with a letter saying they had been "translated" from the "rude songs" of the West. They were widely praised, and Taylor acknowledged authorship in this volume, pretentiously saying that he had attempted "to give a poetical expression to the rude but heroic physical life of the vast desert and mountain region. . . ."[13]

The three original poems that survived to later editions were "El Canelo," one of the first of a long line of Taylor poems about horses; "The Bison Track," which seems to be about hunters pursuing, or being pursued by, a herd of buffalo; and "The Fight of Paso del Mar," about a fatal encounter on a narrow cliffside path between Pablo of San Diego and Bernal of Chino. The "Californian" quality of these poems lies in the setting and in the use of Spanish words; otherwise, the fight of Paso del Mar might have occurred in Palisades Park. The poems are lively, have pronounced rhythms, and could be chanted; but they are not very interesting. This volume displays some skill; there is a variety of meters and stanza forms. But it shows no real maturity—serious striving, anxious hopefulness and desire, but not poetry.

III   A Book of Romances, Lyrics and Songs (*1851*)[14]

A Book of Romances, Taylor's third book of verse, was generally conceded to be the first one worthy of notice; even Stedman said it "gave the first measure of his lyrical powers." Taylor, who felt a new day was dawning for him, insisted that he was "getting into a very different sphere of thought." To George Boker he confided: "I want to make a decent book—something, if possible, which shall put a stop to all this slang about 'promise'; for if I have yet performed nothing, I never shall."[15]

A new day was also dawning in another sense, for this was his first book published by Ticknor, Reed & Fields, *the* publisher in mid-nineteenth-century America. Taylor had assiduously cultivated James T. Fields, who had come to Boston from Portsmouth as a poor boy with literary ambitions similar to Taylor's. He joined Ticknor and Company and rapidly rose to become chief editor and guiding spirit. He had some literary taste and a great deal of congeniality, and he quickly drew to the firm most of the leading New England writers—Emerson, Hawthorne, Longfellow, Lowell, Holmes, Whittier; it became, therefore, prestigious to be published by Ticknor and Fields. For Taylor, it was a great achievement which nonetheless he had earned—by getting Fields's books prominent review space in the *Tribune*, for example.

Nearly all poems in this volume were new, and among them were many which became standard pieces, often reprinted, widely admired, and, in fact, among his best work. "Mon-da-Min," "Love and Solitude," "Hylas," "Kubleh," "The Metempsychosis of the Pine," "The Soldier and the Pard," and "Ariel in the Cloven Pine"—these were called "Romances," a sort of lyric poem with a narrative element. Smyth thought that "Hassan to his Mare" was "among the finest poems on the horse that our literature contains"—which may well be right. Others pointed out that "Ariel in the Cloven Pine," "Sorrowful Music," and "Ode to Shelley" remind one too much of Shelley, from whose influence Taylor never quite freed himself.

"Mon-da-Min, or the Spirit of Maize" (which Taylor said was not about liquor but an Indian deity) was admired by Longfellow, perhaps because it so much resembles Longfellow's own Indian narratives. This poem dramatizes in fifty six-line stanzas a legend from Henry Schoolcraft, the American Indian ethnologist. Osseo, son of a poor Huron Indian chief, wishes he could provide better for the tribe. A celestial shape appears, offering to wrestle:

> But blessings are not free; they do not fall
> In listless hands; by toil the soul must prove
> Its steadfast purpose master over all,
> Before their wings in pomp of coming move;
> Here, wrestling with me, must you overcome,
> In me, the secret,—else, my lips are dumb.
>   (St. 28)

They wrestle for three days, at the end of which the exhausted spirit gives Osseo instructions about how to bury him; if Osseo keeps the place clear of weeds and crows, the result will be knowledge. When these directions are fulfilled, corn grows from the grave; Osseo has brought his people the secret of corn.

The poem, mildly interesting, illustrates one of Taylor's chief faults: it is filled with descriptions of woods, flowers, and animals; and it is "profuse," the word most often used to describe his work. The stanzas are handled well enough, but the poem is simply not remarkable.

"The Soldier and the Pard," a dramatic blank-verse monologue, concerns a soldier of Napoleon in North Africa who falls asleep at an oasis while his comrades march away. Awaking, he finds a leopard staring at him; he is terrified, but the leopard loves the soldier at first sight. Soon, they are getting along well:

> Thus we, in that oasis all alone,
> Sat when the sun went down; the Pard and I,
> Caressing and caressed; and more of love
> And more of confidence between us came.
>   (ll. 124-27)

Unfortunately, however, "Sin will find the way to paradise"; the soldier's infatuation wears off; and one day, when he misunderstands her playfulness, he stabs her to death. Of course, he is guilt-ridden about it, and he tells his audience: "if a man/ Deny this truth she taught me, to his face/ I say he lies: a beast may have a soul" (ll. 241-43).

This story (which was used by Balzac in "A Passion in the Desert") is certainly silly, and Taylor does little to make it believable; but the blank verse is good, flexible, various. Taylor's weakness is essentially imaginative; he doesn't derive from the tale so much as Balzac did; and, if all it shows is that "a beast may have a soul," it is not much above the level of a tract of the Society for the Prevention of Cruelty to Animals.

"Hylas," one of Taylor's most admired poems, is not bad. Its subject is classical, but the language is lush and sonorous. It even has a titillating disrobing scene, like Coleridge's "Christabel"—except that the disrober is a boy. Hylas, who takes a swim one warm afternoon, is enticed beneath the water to drown by the lovely and lonely naiads. Although there is no more to the story, the language is so luxuriant that it remains one of Taylor's best performances.

> . . . and ever closer
> Wound the cold arms, till, climbing to his shoulders,
> Their cheeks lay nestled, while the purple tangles
> Their loose hair made, in silken mesh enwound him,
> Their eyes of clear, pale emerald then uplifting,
> They kissed his neck with lips of humid coral,
> And once again there came a murmur, "Hylas!
> O, Come with us! O, follow where we wander
> Deep down beneath the green, translucent ceiling,—
> Where on the sandy bed of old Scamander
> With cool white buds we braid our purple tresses,
> Lulled by the bubbling waves around us stealing!"
>
> (ll. 77-88)

"Hylas—beautiful Hylas," said his friend Boker. "You do not know how you have advanced in *strength* and finish."[16] Others thought the poem "worthy to stand beside all but the best of Walter Savage Landor."[17] Yet, while skillful, the poem is about nothing important; it has no reverberating echoes or suggestions of larger meaning. It comes close to being "pure poetry," for it is unrelated to anything else, including human experience.

A new Californian ballad in this volume was "The Summer Camp," a poem more concrete and more thoroughly thought out than the earlier ones. After a long trip, some mule riders find a cool shady spot where they are tempted to stay. "Where is the life we led? Whither hath fled/ The turbulent stream that brought us hither?" they say:

> Not in this camp, in these enchanted Trees
> But in ourselves, must lodge the calm we seek,

Ere we can fix it here.
. . . .
Rather set at once
Our faces toward the noisy world again,
And gird our loins for action. Let us go!
(ll. 163-65, 180-82)

The poem illustrates another of Taylor's problems—the persistent echoes of other poets. "Where is the life we led" recalls Shakespeare; "Whither hath fled" sounds like Wordsworth's "Ode to Immortality"; and the idea of the poem resembles that of Tennyson's "Lotus-Eaters." Many critics noted this derivativeness, and the frequent suggestion that his work resembled someone else's greatly annoyed Taylor. Perhaps the trouble was caused by his memory; he once complained that he was unable to forget things he had read.

The "Ode to Shelley" should be noted since it is addressed to Taylor's idol, though Shelley's influence, which dominated his early career, later gave way to Tennyson's. This poem is good imitation Shelley; highly abstract, it asserts that the world needs Shelley. "I too demand thy song," says Taylor; "twin-doomed with thee, to feel the scorn of Wrong/ to worship Beauty as a thing divine!" But, he concludes, things may be better as they are: "Were once thy starry nature given to mine,/ In the one life which would encircle us/ My voice would melt, my soul be lost in thine" (St. 5, ll. 2-4). The poem is well done; and, if one had never read Shelley, one would think more highly of it.

Indeed, most of the poems in this volume are at least well done; for this collection is one of his best. Taylor was concerned that his first book with Ticknor and Fields should not be a financial failure, and he offered to repay Fields for any loss. After some hesitation, Fields replied that the volume had sold "to the extent which leaves the author thereof uncalled upon to pay." But sales were small; the first printing was only one thousand copies, and there is no record of a second.[18]

IV   Poems of the Orient (1854)[19]

Poems of the Orient, published in October, 1854, was Taylor's most popular collection. The chorus of approval that greeted it and the judgments of subsequent critics indicate that it elicited a significant response. One critic who called it a "wonder book" said it was "the highest expression of Taylor's delight in the world."[20] Stedman thought the volume contained "the best work of his purely lyrical period" and was "vivid, spontaneous, harmonious in tone and artistic in execution." Furthermore, he added, "These lyrics are free from moralizing and show little of the influence of Longfellow, which at that time was so visible in American verse; they are poetry uttered for poetry's sake, and with the voice that sings independently."[21] Lowell also praised them, but he cautioned Taylor to "beware of becoming too deeply enamoured of the sensuous in poetry . . . you must not trust too far to your own purity, because few of your readers will be able to match it."[22] Taylor seems to have taken this advice seriously, for he tried in subsequent volumes to reduce his sensuousness.

The book sold well; and Taylor told Boker in December that "the second thousand of my poems is rapidly melting away. The book is considered a decided success." Longfellow, he said, "spoke to me about it in the warmest and kindest manner." Taylor's later critics thought less of the book. Taylor's "true spirit of the east" Beatty described as "distinguished mostly by accelerated heart beats and breathlessness," and his Orientalism consisted chiefly of exotic names.[23]

Most of these poems have died since their time, but a look at a few of the better ones may give a clue to their appeal. The volume contained forty lyrics, plus an introductory poem in which Taylor compares himself with Stoddard. Apollo, he asserted, was the god of Stoddard's verse, while his own was Pan:

> . . . . Blame me not, that I
> Find in the forms of Earth a deeper joy
> Than in the dreams which lured me as a boy,
> And leave the Heavens, where you are wandering still
>   With bright Apollo, to converse with Pan. . . .[24]
>   (St. 4, ll. 30-34)

"The Temptation of Hassan Ben Kaled" is typical of the Oriental poems. It conveys some Arabic flavor, in expressions like "Woe to him whose life casts dirt upon/ The Prophet's word!"; and it is liberally sprinkled with musk, cimeter, myrrh, and royal-blooded steeds. The story concerns Hassan, a street

singer in Cairo, who disappears for two days and later reappears
a more somber man who tells the story of his temptation. He
was invited to a rich man's house by the river, a setting elaborately described:

> . . . oranges that glow
> Like globes of fire, enclosed a heart of snow
> Which thawed not in their flame: like balls of gold
> The peaches seemed, that had in blood been rolled;
> Pure saffron mixed with clearest amber stained
> The apricots; bunches of amethyst
> And sapphire seemed the grapes, so newly kissed
> That still the mist of Beauty's breath remained. . . .
>   (St. 5, ll. 19-26)

Waited on by slaves, he succumbed to the temptations of food,
wine, music, and finally a gorgeous maiden:

> Her hair was braided darkness, but the glance
> Of lightning eyes shot from her countenance,
> And showed her neck, that like an ivory tower
> Rose o'er the twin domes of her marble breast.
>   (St. 8, ll. 9-12)

Later, when he awoke in the street, he felt "the bitter smart/Of
evil knowledge, and the unhealthy lust/ Of sinful pleasure. . . ."
The poem has a moralistic point:

> And from that time I have not dared to curse
> The unrighteous, since the man who seemeth worse
> Than I, may purer be; for, when I fell,
> Temptation reached a loftier pinnacle.
> Therefore, O Man! be Charity thy aim:
> Praise cannot harm, but weigh thy words of blame.
>   (St. 11, ll. 22-27)

The verse is supple and various; the story, vigorous and titillating.
The long passages of sensuous detail about food and music recall
Keats's "The Eve of St. Agnes," and they are not badly done.

In "Amran's Wooing," Amran falls madly in love with the
Sheikh's daughter—"The shrouded graces of her form;/ The
half-seen arm, so round and warm." Naturally, the Sheikh refuses

to give her to him; and, in best Hollywood style, he steals her
and gallops off into the desert, swearing that "no other bed
than mine shall wear/ Her virgin honors. . . ." Then follows a
sensuous passage which may help explain the appeal of these
poems in the mid-nineteenth century:

> By Allah! like a bath of flame
> The seething blood tumultuous came
> From life's hot centre as I drew
> Her mouth to mine; our spirits grew
> Together in one long, long kiss,—
> One swooning, speechless pulse of bliss,
> That, throbbing from the heart's core, met
> In the united lips.
>
> (St. 11, ll. 18-25)

Of course, the Sheikh forgives the lovers when he sees little
Solyman toddling around.

"The Poet in the East" tells how Taylor felt at ease in the
Orient, for "his soul was native/ There":

> All things to him were the visible forms
>   Of early and precious dreams,—
> Familiar visions that mocked his quest
>   Beside the Western streams,
> Or gleamed in the gold of the clouds, unrolled
>   In the sunset's dying beams.
>
> (St. 11)

However, the most famous poem is "The Bedouin Song," and
it is also Taylor's most popular single poem. Set to music many
times, it is supposedly still sung by glee clubs over the nation.
The first of its three stanzas reads:

> From the Desert I come to thee
>   On a stallion shod with fire;
> And the winds are left behind
>   In the speed of my desire.
> Under thy window I stand,
>   And the midnight hears my cry:
> I love thee, I love but thee,
>   With a love that shall not die

Till the sun grows cold,
And the stars are old,
And the leaves of the Judgment
Book unfold!

Though this poem has been called little more than "a pedestrian debauchment of Shelley's 'Indian Serenade',"[25] its popularity was remarkable and immediate. Even as late as 1907 Smyth believed "it would last as long as anything in American Poetry."[26]

Another lyric widely admired was "Daughter of Egypt":

Daughter of Egypt, veil thine eyes!
    I cannot bear their fire;
Nor will I touch with sacrifice
    Those altars of Desire.
For they are flames that shun the day
    And their unholy light
Is fled from natures gone astray
    In passion and in night.

The second stanza repeats the idea of beauty tempting men to sin; the narrator fears that he might "in the black waves of thy hair/ My struggling manhood drown!" This poem has been called superior to many Elizabethan lyrics because it presents "the moral nature recoiling upon the passionate and holding it in suppression."[27]

There are other interesting lyrics in this volume—about horses, for instance. It may be hard to believe that these lines—"Bend thy forehead now, to take my kisses/ Lift in love thy dark and splendid eye"—refer to a horse, but they do. Others are about wine, the wisdom of the prophets, the beauty of the sun, the garden of Irem, and Persian boys. Taylor's closing remarks, in "L'Envoi," are:

I found, among those Children of the Sun,
    The cipher of my nature,—the release
Of baffled powers, which else had never won
    That free fulfillment, whose reward is peace.
                                        (St. XV)

Poems of the Orient is an interesting volume. While there is too much straining after colorfulness and excitement and while the titillations are—to a modern reader—rather tame, the book was daring enough for its time. In fact, it was different enough from the pallidness of Genteel literature to attract attention. Furthermore, Taylor convinces the reader that, while his idea of Eastern life may be superficial, as he understood it, he liked it. This life, different from an American's, demands attention and respect, he says. As for accuracy, that matters less; Taylor records how he experienced the East.

These poems are not free of moralizing, but the moral is not obtrusive and is consistent with the material. This verse is zestful, vigorous, and athletic; and it has a lyrical quality which, while not of the highest order, is nonetheless genuine. "Song" was Taylor's synonym for poetry; and he emphasized too much the musical side of verse; but he could write lyrics and ballads which, if they had few memorable lines, were nonetheless effective.

The collection also contained a separate section of non-Oriental poems that concerned Taylor's grief at the death of his wife. And, occasionally, one finds in Taylor's verse an oddly interesting poem which no one seems to have noticed. Such a one is "An Answer"—a poem that seems almost modern in its brevity, its simplicity of diction, and its cryptic quality:

> You call me cold: you wonder why
> The marble of a mien like mine
> Gives fiery sparks of Poesy,
> Or softens at Love's touch divine.
>
> Go, look on Nature, you will find
> It is the rock that feels the sun:
> But you are blind,—and to the blind
> The touch of ice and fire is one.

V Poems of Home and Travel (*1855*)[28]

One year after *Poems of the Orient*, Taylor published *Poems of Home and Travel*, a volume drawn from his previous two. With *Poems of the Orient*, this volume constituted a sort of collected edition. In compiling it, he rejected much of his poetry; for, he said, these two books contained all the poetry he was willing to acknowledge. *Poems of Home and Travel* contains sixty-six poems grouped under such headings as "Romances and Lyrics," "Californian Ballads and Poems," "Rhymes of Travel, and Early Poems," and "Later Poems," headings which were by and large retained throughout subsequent editions.

This volume contains only twelve new poems; and, generally, these are quite conventional and usually sentimental poems. "Wind and Sea" is a Shelley-esque lyric reminiscent of "The Clouds":

> The Sea is a jovial comrade,
>   He laughs wherever he goes;
> His merriment shines in the dimpling lines
>   That wrinkle his hale repose. . . .
>   (ll. 1-4)

"My Dead" mourns the poet's youth in the traditional manner (he was thirty at the time). "Studies for Pictures" is a sequence of four lyrics in which the domestic theme appears for the first time:

> My neighbor at his window stands,
> His youngest baby in his hands;
> The others seek his tender kiss,
> And one sweet woman crowns his bliss.
>   (I, St. 4)

In "A Fantasy," a forest maiden blowing a silver horn appears as the unattainable ideal:

> For my touch would chill your pulses,
>   And my kiss make dim your eye,
> And the horn will first be silent
>   In the hour that you shall die.
>   (St. 9)

"The Mariners" praises sailors for their courage, fortitude, innocence, and ruggedness:

> Say that they curse, if you will,
>   That the tavern and harlot possess their gains;
> On the surface floats what they do of ill—
>   At the bottom the manhood remains.
>   (St. 10)

These poems are good samples of Taylor's verse in that they are competent without being in any way remarkable. There is hardly anything memorable about them, yet they are readable enough. Though Taylor continued to write poems, he did not publish another volume of poetry for seven years; his energies were absorbed by travel, journalism, lecturing, and building his house at Kennett Square. Indeed, not until he moved into "Cedarcroft" in 1860 did he return to writing poetry extensively.

VI The Poet's Journal (*1862*)[29]

Taylor produced *The Poet's Journal* rapidly after settling into his new house; indeed, his wife said that nearly all the lyrical portion was written in one month. "I am in a fury of writing," he told a friend, "and cannot stop,—cannot do or think of anything else."[30] Unfortunately, it took two years for the book to be published. Fields was worried about the approaching election and the threat of civil war; and, although Taylor argued that "My name is still well before the public, and my other books sell encouragingly,"[31] the book did not appear until the fall of 1862 when Taylor was in Russia. When it did appear, Taylor was angered by Fields's advertising: the book was personal, and the publisher had emphasized its autobiographical quality. Said Taylor: "Why, oh why, did you issue such an advertisement? . . . The 'Journal' is not entirely the record of my own experience, though that certainly forms its basis. Ernest is only half myself, and Edith is only one fourth my wife. The story is a mixture of truth and poetry, and was never intended to be put forth as a personal record."[32]

However, the interest the poem aroused was due largely to these autobiographical suggestions; and criticism of its other qualities was not profuse. Even Stedman said that "Its chief interest is found in a revelation of the author's heart."[33] Smyth's view was similar: "The great sorrow that had overshadowed his young life in the death of his first wife, and had driven him to foreign lands to ease the restless anguish of his heart, now found its voice in many poems that utter the sad experience he had known. . . . He gathered the recollections of his moods, and told the story of his voyage from pain to peace . . . . He had melted his sorrows and had run them into a mould from which

he lifted a form of beauty that was a benefaction to the
world . . . ."[34] The entire poem glorified "family love, in its
wholeness and its wholesomeness."

Taylor, who was fond of the book, always put it in the fore-
front of his subsequent collections. It also marked a turn in his
work, for it is an approach to the long narrative poem. Its
thirty-five lyrics are set into a framework which gives not only
form but also a sense of relatedness to the whole. The subject
is a man's slowly finding his way out of the despair caused by
the death of his loved one through a new love that results in
marriage and a child. The poem moves, therefore, from despair
to hope to happiness in domestic life.

Taylor's frequent objection to biographical readings of his
verse is puzzling because a great deal of his verse is autobiographical. Even a simple lyric may have some relevance to
an actual event in the manner of Romantic poets generally. For
example, the preface to *The Poet's Journal*, an eight-stanza lyric
titled "The Return of the Goddess," would not mean much unless
the reader knew that Taylor hadn't written much poetry for
five years.

The narrative setting of the work concerns the long-delayed
return home of brother Ernest, who now has a wife and baby.
The homebody brother, Phillip, anxiously awaits his return:

> Ten years had passed since I had touched his hand,
> And felt upon my lips the brother-kiss
> That shames not manhood,—years of quiet bliss
> To me, fast-rooted on paternal land,
> Mated, yet childless.
>
> (ll. 82-86)

After his arrival, Ernest narrates the harrowing tale of his
journey from darkness to light, or "how I lost that sorest load/ I
started with, and came to dwell at last/ In the House Beautiful."
The poem is divided into three "evenings," the first of which
contains ten lyrics with such titles as "Darkness," "The Dead
March," and "The Voice of the Tempter," which explain Ernest's
feelings at the loss of his first love. In "Darkness," for example,
he says:

> And every gift that Life to me had given
> Lies at my feet, in useless fragments trod:

> There is no justice or in Earth or Heaven:
> There is no pity in the heart of God.
> (St. 5)

The "Voice of the Tempter" tells the narrator to forget and to take the path of pleasant vice. The picture of despair in these poems is reasonably effective, but it is overdone and highly abstract. There are few concrete images; everything is vague, misty, moody; and the result, despite the genuineness of Taylor's feeling, is more rhetoric than anything else. The dangers of abstract imagery may also be seen in "A Symbol," in which the meaninglessness of Time's passage is presented as a chain gang. In the second stanza, Time—long past his prime—is confusingly described as the incestuous father of the felons. The image shifts in stanza three, where nature seems asleep and indifferent: "The Forests fain would groan,/ But, silenced into stone,/ Crouch, in the dull blue vapors round them thrown." Surely the image of forests turned to stone and crouching is difficult to imagine. And the whole poem ends in a pointless affirmation: "O light, more drear than gloom!/ Than death more dead such bloom:/ Yet life—yet life—shall burst this gathering doom!" These are bad lines, and they are so not only because of the difficult inversion in the second one.

The first evening ends with a conventional religious song by Ernest's wife, Edith: "We are sinful, Thou art holy:/ Thou are mighty, we are lowly:/ Let us reach Thee, climbing slowly" (St. 3). Much the same process is followed on the second evening. Ernest recites ten more lyrics, showing signs of possible hope. "Atonement" for example, reads:

> If thou hadst died at midnight,
>   I had ceased to bid thee stay,
> Hearing the feet of the Father
>   Leading His child away.
> . . . .
> But the cruel sun was shining
>   In the cold and windy sky,
> And Life, with his mocking voices,
>   Looked in to see thee die.
> (St. 3, 5)

(This poem actually contains eight more stanzas, which add
very little.) In "Churchyard Roses," the poet becomes melodramatic:

> And down upon that trampled grave
>   In recklessness my body cast:
> "Give back the life I could not save,
>   Or give deliverance from the past!"
>   (St. 7)

Ernest ends the second evening with dewy eyes, as do his
listeners.

On the third evening, festivities begin with the appearance
of Ernest's child, "A darling boy, to both his parents true,—/ With
father's brow, and mother's eyes of blue." Phillip is pained
because he hasn't a child, but he still has hope. Ernest says his
poems will end on this evening:

> Because the gift of Song was chiefly lent
> To give consoling music for the joys
> We lack, and not for those which we possess:
> I now no longer need that gift. . . .
>   (ll. 106-109)

This section contains sixteen lyrics which are more cheerful
and optimistic and—it must be admitted—more sodden. In
"Questions," the new love is introduced:

> I see her, hear her, daily, nightly:
>   My secret dreams around her move,
> Still nearer drawn in sweet attraction;—
>   Can this be love?
>   (St. 2)

In "The Vision," he sees the ghost of his early love and asks:

> "Canst thou forgive me, Angel mine,"
>   I cried; "that Love at last beguiled
> My heart to build a second shrine?
> See, still I kneel and weep at thine,
> But I am human, thou divine!"
>   Still silently she smiled.
>   (St. IV)

She forgives him, of course, thus clearing the way for the new love. Other titles like "Before the Bridal" and "Possession" speak for themselves. "Under the Moon" deals with the actual consummation but, of course, in highly abstract terms:

> I see you, darling, at my side:
> I clasp you closer, in sacred pride.
> I shut my eyes, my senses fail,
> Becalmed by Night's ambrosial gale.
> (St. V, ll. 1-4)

It has been said that no Genteel poet could be trusted with a baby; but neither could he be trusted with a mother, wife, or young girl without losing his critical taste. Especially did legal, domestic love turn them into jelly. But this last evening ends as the others have, with a song from Edith: "Though Thy ways we cannot see,/ All is just that comes from Thee."

The relation of the volume to Taylor's own experience is obvious. His sense of guilt at the death of Mary Agnew and his subsequent remarriage are exorcised in these poems as best he can do it. As a celebration of domestic love, the volume nearly smothers its subject; but some individual lyrics are respectably done. Taylor was not uncritical of his own work, as can be seen in the following remarks to Stoddard: "Your criticism . . . is correct, and I wish you had made it when you read the MSS. The poems, as a whole, lack distinct form, and I could easily have corrected this fault. I could very much improve them now. I think I am a better poet than ever before; at least, I see my own deficiencies more clearly. I have lost, maybe, a little lyric swing, but I had an overplus of it at the start."[35] Although Taylor sees their fault as one of form, to a modern reader the fault is an excessive indulgence in feeling and sentimentalism as he approaches love and children. What he really lacks, perhaps, is refined feeling as well as subtlety of language.

VII   The Poems of Bayard Taylor (*1864*)

Taylor achieved the dignity of a first collected edition, *The Poems of Bayard Taylor,* in the famous Blue and Gold Series of Ticknor and Fields. This volume of 419 pages contains a hundred and seventy poems—not a bad quantity of work for a man not yet forty. He began the volume with *The Poet's Journal* and followed with *Poems of the Orient*. Next came a classical narrative, "Passing the Sirens," followed by "Romances and Lyrics," "Californian Ballads and Poems," "Earlier Poems," and finally eight new poems (most about the Civil War) labeled "Since 1861." The first two parts were as originally published, but there was considerable shifting around of the romances and lyrics.

This collected edition was the only one Taylor compiled, for he died in 1878 before he was able to make another. Although the Cabinet Edition appeared the following year, 1865, its contents were identical with the Blue and Gold. The final collection was made by his friend George Boker in 1880; it followed largely the same sequence, though Boker omitted many poems under all headings and added the later narratives.

VIII   The Picture of St. John (*1866*)[36]

Taylor had a strong interest in pictorial art; he frequently sketched, and he painted in both oils and watercolor. He also had a number of artist friends: Jarvis McEntee, Eastman Johnson, and Edward Hicks. *The Picture of St. John* is about an artist, and it was dedicated to his artist friends; however, it was aimed at his literary friends. Taylor, who thought highly of it, believed it would earn for him a substantial place among the country's poets—as his own account of the writing of the poem indicates:

. . . .I commenced "The Picture of St. John" in June, 1850, with no very clear conception, and no more serious purpose than to write a narrative poem of love and sorrow, with an artist as the hero. . . . When, in 1854, I recommenced, a vague feeling that the theme contained material which I was not mature enough to use made me desist. . . .About the end of March, 1863. . . .I resumed this poem as an experiment. I soon discovered, by the new and more important shape which it assumed in my mind, that the time had come when, if ever, it should be written. . .Whatever faults or merits the poem may have, it is *my own*, unsuggested by any circumstance, and uninfluenced by any creation of others. It closes the second stage of my development as a poet, and is already colored, towards the end, by the growth of what I feel to be a new (and probably the last) stage of my poetic faculty. . . .I feel and know that it is beyond all comparison the one good thing which I have produced.[37]

In all his comments about his own work, Taylor returned to the four points made here. First, the poem is his own, it is original; for he had been much bothered by criticism that he lacked originality. Second, the poem is the beginning of a new stage of poetic growth; he never defines what the stages are, though generally he thought he was becoming more restrained. Third, this poem (any poem) is the best thing he has done. Fourth, he doesn't care (by implication) what the public thinks; what other poets think is what matters. "I am writing this time to establish myself alongside the truly illustrious names in American literature," he wrote Boker; "I am working to become one with Bryant and Longfellow, with Lowell and Whittier. They shall appraise it."[38]

As for originality, subsequent readers have noted various thematic and linguistic sources in this poem that range from Coleridge's "The Ancient Mariner" to Browning. One critic, who traced its principal incidents to "Oberon" by the German author Wieland, added that even the names of the characters are similar.[39] These similarities could hardly be coincidence, but they could indicate Taylor's remarkable memory working without his conscious knowledge. And, as for Taylor's insistence on constant growth, it is puzzling. Certainly, he mastered many techniques of his art; but no one has been able to identify the stages Taylor felt he was passing through. One noticeable thing is that he is now writing long poems; but even Beatty remarked that "the higher stage of his development Taylor spoke of is imperceptible."[40]

At least Taylor's hopes for the good opinion of his fellow-poets were fulfilled. He informed them of his progress, sent a copy and a note to each, and they delivered the expected praise. Taylor's years of cultivating James T. Fields (as their publisher and the center of the group), his frequent pilgrimages to New England to wine and dine with them, and his prompt praise of their latest books all had good results; they could hardly do otherwise than respond with praise. Of course, his closer friends also sent their compliments, but it was praise from the best-known poets that Taylor really desired. The poem, he told a friend, "has at last procured me admission into the small company of American poets who have some chance of life.

. . . It will always be liked, I think, by the few who make
fame for an author."[41]

For Longfellow had written to him: "You have written a
great poem,—noble, sustained, and beautiful from beginning to
end." Whittier: "I marvel at its exquisite finish and beauty. It
is a poem for poets and painters." Lowell: "No American poem
except the 'Golden Legend' can match it in finish and sustained
power." Holmes: "I think it must be an American gift, to unite
such different powers as those which belong to the traveler
and the poet." Bryant: "I congratulate you on having produced
the best of your longer poems"[42] (since it was Taylor's *first*
long poem, this comment is puzzling).

The Picture of St. John is divided into four books and the
poetry is in ottava rima. The first two parts contain ninety-one
stanzas each; the third, eighty-seven; the fourth, eighty-six—a
total of two thousand eight hundred and forty lines. Taylor tried
to avoid monotony by varying the rhyme scheme, and he claimed
over seventy variations. Egon, the artist character of the book,
is a poor boy whose "infant frame" is informed by a "nimbler
life." He learned to paint in Venice, but not as he wants;
when he paints a fisherman as St. John the Evangelist, the
picture is too sensual:

> So keen with life, so marked in every line
> With unideal nature, none had guessed
> The dream that cheered me and the faith that led;
> But human all I would have made divine!
> (Bk. I, St. XXX, ll. 5-8)

Unable to paint the ideal beauty he aspires to record, he sur-
renders to a sensuous life. "Two spirits dwell in us," he says,
repeating one of his favorite ideas, "one chaste and pale,/ A still
recluse, whose garments know no stain/. . . . The other bound-
ing to her cymbal's clang,/ A bold Bacchante, panting with
the race/ Of joy." While the artist is on his way to Florence one
day, he sees a girl as fair as his "Madonna-dream." Later, in
the market, an elderly man hires him to paint his daughter, who
of course is the same girl; but she is to be unwillingly married to
a wealthy nobleman. Trying to paint her, Egon is shaken with
emotion: "The pencil fell; I turned,/ And with imploring eyes

and tears that burned/ Sank in despairing silence at her feet."
They agree to meet that night in the garden; and "She came!
a stealthy, startled, milk-white fawn,/ Thridding the tangled
bloom." She exacts a promise: " 'Fail me not,' she said,/ And
clung the closer,—'God is overhead./ And hears you.' " At the
consummation of their love, Taylor switches to his most abstract
language:

> With cautious feet, in dewy sandals shod,
> And sidelong look, the perfumed Hours went by;
> Until the azure darkness of the sky
> Withered aloft, and shameless Morning trod
> Her clashing bells. . . .
>
> (Bk. II, St. XIX)

The lovers run away to his home in Bavaria, where he continues
to paint; but his palette is now spread with "colors dull and
raw." By spring, she is pregnant; and the pregnancy is thus
described: "Between our hearts, embracing both, there stole/ A
silent Presence, like to that which reigns/ In Heaven, when
God another world ordains" (Bk. II, St. LXXIV). Naturally,
Clelia resembles the Madonna; and the baby a "stray lamb of
heaven."

The boy is delightful, and Egon wants to paint him as St.
John, as Ganymede, and as St. George; for his artistic interests
lie entirely in painting abstractions. Meanwhile, Clelia, who
begins to fade, soon dies; and Egon takes his son back to Italy.
He tries to paint him as St. John, but he has to stop frequently
to kiss him— "o'er and o'er,—/ Cheek, bosom, limbs." But the
boy is kidnapped by his grandfather, Pandolfo; and, when Egon
finds him, the old Marchese, attacking him, accidentally kills
the boy. Death reconciles the two, who "clung like drowning
men beneath the wave."

The rest of the poem describes, abstractly, Egon's development
as a painter. He is depressed: why is the artist more sensitive
than others if it only means he suffers more? He decides that Art
is a Devilhood, and he begins to draw ribald pictures and
monsters. But a vision of his son as St. John sends him back
to work on the portrait, while a "solemn presence" that appears
berates his weakness for ten stanzas. Sounding like the voice from
the whirlwind, it says the Artist is

>   . . . the flag of truce
> Between the warring worlds of soul and sense:
> By neither mastered, holding both apart,
> Or blending in a newer excellence,
> He weds the haughty brain and yearning heart.
>   (Bk. IV, St. LXVII)

The advice improves Egon's attitude, whose soul then "quired anew the world-old human song,—/ Accepting patience and forgetting wrong!" When his joy in Art returns, it is purified by "meek acceptance in the place of pride."

Far from being original, this story is a perfectly conventional Romantic tale, though the idea of a man achieving some deeper understanding of life by experiencing life's sorrows is perfectly respectable, if trite. Smyth professes to admire the poem; Beatty, however, thought it a "sadly overworked story" containing "the entire fixed series of conventions—which the Romantic school has employed for decades."[43] And Taylor's poem is constantly excessive. Certainly parents love their children, but how many grab them to kiss their "cheeks, bosom, and limbs"? How many inept grandfathers stab their favorites accidentally? In addition, much of Taylor's trouble lies in an inflated, abstract rhetoric which he evidently thought poetry should have. Time passes "in dewy sandals shod"; a baby is "a silent Presence"; women are madonnas or "budding, spotless maids"; legal union is "consecrated." One cannot imagine an idea in these terms; and, since the language is meaningless, one feels the author isn't really *seeing* anything.

Behind unreal language lie unreal conceptions. If one sees a child as a "stray lamb of Heaven," one does not know much about children; if purity and innocence are the only qualities one values in women, then one wonders about one's sense. Of course, these concepts are drawn from Christian mythology; but a poet is supposed to know when language is dead, for language is his business. Taylor cannot conceive of language or ideas that have not been used by generations of previous poets. He can imagine that he *ought* to conceive such, and hence one has his assertions of originality and new growth. But these are delusions, for one finds nothing new in this volume except, perhaps, the "70 variations" of the rhyme scheme.

The poem is, however, technically skillful. Beatty thought it "very smooth," but "its language uniformly fails to approximate the inevitability of great verse."[44] To Smyth, its chief defects were "immaturity of conception and juvenility of phrase."[45] The poem has indeed much pleasant language, it contains many elaborate descriptions, and it presents a view of love common at the time. For a modern reader, however, it is simply unreal. "The cardinal fact about *The Picture* now," said Beatty, "is that it is dead to us."[46]

IX   *The Masques*

Taylor wrote two masques—*The Golden Wedding* (1868), and *The Masque of the Gods* (1872).[47] The first work was, as the title suggests, a theatrical prepared by Taylor to celebrate his parents' fiftieth wedding anniversary, and he had it privately printed by Lippincott in a fancy format for presentation to them. Its chief interest lies in some tipped-in photographs of Taylor's parents, of "Cedarcroft," of Taylor himself, and of his two friends Stoddard and Boker. The masque itself (in which a role as attendant fairy is held by his daughter, Lilian) is mercifully brief, only eleven pages.

Between *The Picture of St. John* and Taylor's next poetical volume his energies were devoted largely to the translation of *Faust*, Part I, which was issued in late 1870, and to Part II, which was published the following March. *The Masque of the Gods* (1872) was written shortly after *Faust* was completed, and it bears some relation to (and a lot of influence from) that work. Taylor's wife remarked that his work on *Faust* "deepened the growing tendency of his mind to occupy itself with the large movements of thought.... It was only the due expression of his growth, therefore, when ... he sat down and in four days wrote, almost at white heat, his poem, 'The Masque of the Gods.' "[48]

Taylor himself explained the meaning of the poem, or at least the meaning he intended:

The gradual development of man's conception of God: first, a colossal reflection of human powers and passions, mixed with the dread inspired by the unknown forces of nature; then, the idea of Law (Elohim), of Order and Beauty and Achievement (love and Apollo),

and of the principles of Good and Evil (Persian), and of the Divine
Love (Christ).

But over all is the ONE supreme Spirit, yet unnamed, and whom
men only now begin to conceive of,—the God of whom all previous
gods have only faint and various reflections,—to whom Christ is still
nearest, but who was also felt, more or less dimly, in all creeds.[49]

Taylor's letters about *The Masque of the Gods* repeat views
expressed before. It "will either make or break me," he told a
friend; to another, he asserted that it was "something 'new and
strange,' and may make a 'sea-change' with me, so far as the
critics are concerned."[50] He was delighted at a review in a German periodical which called it "one of the most remarkable and
original poems ... written in America."[51] Once again (despite
its obvious debt to Goethe) he insisted on its originality: "at
last ... I have some qualities which are my own, not simulated
or borrowed."

The Masque of the Gods, only forty pages long, has three
scenes. The first occurs on the high tableland of Pamere at midnight; speaking are the Rocks, Caverns, Serpents, and Wolves;
then Odin, Perun, and Baal, A Voice from Space, and Man.
Man remarks that he had worshiped these gods, "But they forget,
they perish or desert us,/ Too weak, without us, to become immortal." In Scene II, which occurs in a Doric temple above the
Aegean Sea, the Trees, Rivers, Mountains, and Sea speak; then
Jove, Elohim, Ormuzd, Ahriman, Apollo, Immanuel, and Man
again. The gods debate their own relative value. Scene III opens
in "a vast landscape," with a chorus of Spirits singing:

> The Deities die when their work is done.
> But the mantle of One is wide to enfold us,
> The heart of One is a Father's to love us,
> The spirit of One shall lift us and hold!
>   (ll. 15-18)

Each of the abstractions defines his views; and when Man comments that he doesn't understand, the Voice replies, in closing,
"Wait! Ye shall know."

The poem, highly pretentious, is stupefyingly dull. It is possible to have abstract spirits speaking if they say something
and if the author has a philosophical mind. But the essential

statement of this poem could be put into a sentence; Taylor simply did not have the philosophical depth for this sort of thing. The poem does represent an advanced religious view; for Taylor to suggest that Christianity is an incomplete conception of God was daring. But the fact remains that the poem hardly registers on the mind, even after repeated readings.

Nonetheless, some liked it. Longfellow said, "I am delighted to see you taking so high a flight"; Whittier also sent congratulations. Newspaper notices were "pure glorification." Thomas Bailey Aldrich liked it, John Osgood liked it, Holmes liked it, his wife liked it. Yet, there is a hint of Taylor's disappointment: the public didn't like it. "If this public won't accept my better work, I must wait until a new one grows up," he said. *The Masque of the Gods* faded quickly: it didn't sell; and Taylor stopped referring to it rather early.

The Masque of the Gods was Taylor's first drama, though of course it is unactable. But it does show that his work on *Faust* turned his interests in this direction; for two of his next three poems were also dramas.

X Lars: A Pastoral of Norway (*1873*)[52]

Taylor's first mention of *Lars* was on October 28, 1872, when he said that in three or four weeks he had written the first two parts and was working on the third; he estimated the total would be twenty-one hundred lines. (His estimates were uncannily accurate; the completed poem had twenty-one hundred and thirty-five lines.) When he finished it in November, he described it as a narrative poem with "a touching and quite original story" which was "not only highly moral, but religious!!!" Once again, he insisted on its newness and originality.

Very important to Taylor was the fact that *Lars* was his first poem to be published in England. Some of his books had been available there; but, aside from his *Faust* translation, the only other poem of his published there was his last one, *Prince Deukalion*. Unfortunately, *Lars* was not very successful; and Taylor remarked a year later that it had sold only a hundred and eight copies in England; as a result, he saw his chances for "impartial recognition" there quietly disappearing.

Explaining the poem to Whittier, Taylor said he had "brought

Quaker peace and Berserker rage into conflict, and given the
triumph to the former." To another Quaker friend, he added
that, "if the Quakers are not satisfied with my presentation of
them and their peaceful creed, they do not deserve a place in our
literature."[53] The story begins in a village in Norway where
Brita, a frivolous young lady, "glossy as a mating bird," is loved
by two local men, Per and Lars. At a wedding party, they clash
over Brita; and they fight in accord with traditions of the "old
Berserker madness in their blood." When Lars kills Per, Brita
realizes belatedly that Per was the man she wanted.

Lars goes to America to find his ancestors, but he can find no
trace of them:

> . . . .The name of Leif
> Who should remember? Do we call to mind,
> Years afterward, the clover-head we plucked
> Some morn of June, and smelled, and threw away?
> But when we find a life erased and lost
> Beneath the multitude's unsparing feet,—
> A life so clearly beating yet for us
> In blood and memory,—comes a sad surprise.
> (pp. 317-18)

Lars is hired by a Quaker farmer at the behest of his daughter,
Ruth. However, neighbor Abner Cloud, who covets Ruth, is
jealous; he is rich, "rigid in the sect," and goads Lars at every
chance. One day, goaded beyond endurance, Lars, in a rage,
accidentally knocks down Ruth's father. Despite the accident,
her father asks forgiveness for Lars; he replies: "I see the truth,
but in my heart the lamp/ Is barely lighted, any wind may
quench./ Bear with me still, be helpful, that I live!" (326-27).

Lars and Ruth agree to marry. But, says Taylor, "Love's history, as Life's, is ended not/ By marriage." Lars, who still remem-
bers his guilt from Norway, wants to take the Quaker word to
his own people. Ruth joins him in his mission, and they found a
Quaker colony at Arendal—"a brotherhood/ Of earnest seekers
for the light." But Lars must face the revenge of Per's brother,
Thorsten; when he challenges Lars, Lars refuses to fight; he
wants to "end this bloody custom so,/ In all the land." His
superior moral virtue and Ruth's goodness persuade Thorsten;
and they all return to Arendal:

Here, now, they fade. The purpose of their lives
Was lifted up, by something over life,
To power and service. Though the name of Lars
Be never heard, the healing of the world
Is in its nameless saints. Each separate star
Seems nothing, but a myriad scattered stars
Break up the Night, and make it beautiful.

(p. 341)

Lars must be accounted one of Taylor's better poems. The story is reasonably interesting, and there are some good fight scenes. Characterizations are not very strong, but Lars and Brita are well done; Ruth, like most of Taylor's good women, is too good to be true. Best of all is Taylor's easy and flexible blank verse, as the examples show.

Since Quaker life and beliefs are in their nature unexciting, peace, nonviolence, and the inner light are hard to dramatize. Taylor does not make them interesting, and he has wisely not concentrated on them. Yet, the triumph of peaceful principles Taylor regarded as a victory for progress. *Lars* is not a great poem; but it is well sustained as a narrative, and is not loaded with description. It is a competent piece of work, and one of his best because free from too much sentimentality. Naturally, Taylor's wife thought it a "rhythmically beautiful, picturesque tale." Stedman, more critical, thought that in *Lars*, Taylor had a subject "quite within his powers, and realized his ideal.... This blank-verse poem is a delightful production."[54] On the other hand, *Lars* has not escaped unscathed; Beatty thought its verse "uninspired," and the account of the Quakers "only slightly interesting."[55]

But Taylor was depressed because a chorus of praise did not rise from his friends, except for Whittier—to whom the poem was dedicated. Why is a mystery; but a year after its appearance, Taylor complained that "of a dozen intimate literary friends in New York and Boston, only three have sent me a word of congratulations about *Lars*"[56]—a lack of approval that was terrible for a man who lived on the praise of friends. On the other hand, he had some consolation. At Kennett Square in 1874, his neighbors held a basket picnic in his honor. The chairman "expressed the thanks of Hockessin to the author of *Lars*, because he had not only immortalized the idyllic beauty of the valley, but also given poetic expression to the spirit of Quaker thought and principle."[57] Taylor, overwhelmed, thanked his neighbors "In a voice vibrating with emotion," for "a day which will stand in my memory bathed in its own solemn and sacred light."[58] Later he wrote to a friend: "All the recognition I craved in vain was poured upon me at once. For three hours I had to keep myself, by desperate force of will, from crying like a baby."[59] This welcome from his neighbors with whom he had so often fought was one of the nicest things that had happened to him.

XI   The Prophet: A Tragedy (1874)[60]

Much of Taylor's work was so similar to that of his contemporaries that the reader is sometimes baffled. He was not a plagiarist, but echoes of other people's work in his poems were persistent. He once told Longfellow how similar one of his poems was to one of Longfellow's, assuring him it was a coincidence; he wrote a similar letter to Whittier. When Taylor and Stoddard once published poems on a similar topic, Taylor said they had three or four expressions in common. His relations with Stoddard were once strained by The Echo Club because Stoddard had mentioned the idea to him, but Taylor published it first.

Something like this incident occurred with The Prophet. In conversation, Thomas Bailey Aldrich had "sketched a drama which he meant to write some day with the Mormon superstition for an historic basis." Taylor was paralyzed, for he was also planning such a drama. However, he said nothing but later wrote Aldrich: "When you suggested to me the 'Seven Mormon Wives' in the street, I had already my plan nearly complete, and it cost me an effort not to tell you so."[61] We must accept his account, but the number and the variety of these coincidences remain provocative.

About The Prophet, Taylor made his usual assertions: it was the result of years of thought, it was his best work ("vastly higher than Lars"), it was fresh and original, and it "was a poem to make or break a reputation." The Prophet has five acts and thirty-five scenes; its hero is David Starr, a New England farm boy with serious religious leanings. Urged to repent at a camp meeting, he blithely asks:

> For what should I repent? Why pray as these
> Who cry from secret consciousness of sin?

> I never let a fault against me stand
> For day of settlement, then balanced all
> By pleading bankrupt, only to begin
> A fresh account. . . .
>
> (Act I, Sc. II)

David is hooted out of the meeting for his arrogance; but when his friends urge him to preach, he goes into the wilderness, hoping for a sign, which turns out to be a supply of food left (unknown to him) by Rhoda, his beloved. He soon picks up a devoted follower in scheming Nimrod Kraft. Two years later, they arrive in the West, the "promised land," and found a new church. With time, however, David (now married to Rhoda) is attracted to another woman, Livia; and the ruling Council of Twelve displays signs of ambition.

Otherwise, things in the New Jerusalem are unexciting. New growth is needed, and (although the verse becomes murky) polygamy is proposed. The council approves the idea; for, as one member states,

> The law we pray for gives new power to man,
> Takes old reproach from woman, multiplies
> Inheritors of truth, as born therein,
> And heals perversions that distress the world.
>
> (Act. III, Sc. 3)

Rhoda now reveals that she had set out the food in the wilderness. With his trust in his own miraculous powers thus shaken, David struggles with himself: "The flock I lead/ Is fooled by me, as I have fooled myself!" Livia, however, arranges another miraculous "sign"; and as they embrace, Rhoda searches the Bible for prohibition against multiple marriages.

The new policy is announced, and secrecy is demanded; but dissenters betray the polygamists to outsiders. Kraft has the informers murdered and assumes power, while David, dallying with Livia, becomes indecisive. Kraft hopes to evade prosecution by suppressing evidence; Livia wants to fight with the Gentiles: "The top of life,/ Methinks, is action, when the field is broad;/ For power of nature cannot truly be,/ Till it is proved on others." The sheriff is met with gunfire; and when David runs out with a truce flag, he is mortally wounded. After a few kind words to Rhoda, he dies; but Kraft has the last words: "Zion lives, and shall be strong, through me!" As the curtain falls, he snatches the ark from the altar and escapes.

Like much of Taylor's work, *The Prophet* is mildly interesting without being either moving or perceptive. The weakening of a religious man's force by the corruptions of the world and the institutionalization of a religious impulse are good ideas. But, unfortunately, David Starr is not very complex, though Taylor evidently intended him to be a Hamlet figure. A second fault is the precipitating factor of the action. Taylor sees polygamy as a nadir of morality and as an excuse for lust. Starr's real motive is his desire for Livia and his boredom with marriage to Rhoda. Of course, self-deception is somewhat tragic; but a man whose lust makes him see polygamy as noble is hardly tragic. In this instance, Genteel values have vitiated literary ones.

Taylor, who spent much time explaining his poem, sometimes claimed it had nothing to do with the Mormons; at other times, he admitted that their history formed the background. But he alleged that it cut "the fossilized Orthodox to the heart no less than the Mormons." Perhaps he referred to Starr's insistence on personal inspiration (which was somewhat Quakerish). However, the orthodox probably found little in the poem except reinforcement of their view that faiths like Mormonism are merely eccentric covers for dishonest motives.

Taylor believed that the plot of this poem had "the universal human element" but that readers were misled by the Mormon trappings; therefore, the "main lesson of the drama" was not understood. In an analysis Taylor wrote for a German newspaper, he said his prototype was not Joseph Smith, the founder of Mormonism, but the Reverend Edward Irving, founder of a Scottish sect: "Irving taught the continued bestowal of miraculous powers upon devout Christians, as they were given by Paul to the members of the churches he founded. . . . Starr's . . . unquestioning acceptance of a doctrine . . . —that the Bible is not only divine, but that every word in it was written from the direct dictation of the Holy Spirit—is the power which impels him: this is the fate which makes the tragedy of his life inevitable. . . ."[62] This statement suggests that Starr's belief in the Bible is the source of the tragedy; if so, it must be the only tragedy in existence about literalmindedness.

Commentators generally have not expressed a high opinion of *The Prophet*. The one exception was Smyth, who thought Starr a "fine idealist" and not "a vulgar sensualist" like the Mormon Joseph Smith. To Beatty, the poem was uninspired; to Stedman, its material was unpoetic: the Mormons furnished only "a store of clap-trap to melodramatic playwrights." This criticism reminds one that Taylor had used a "popular" subject: Americans of the time were scandalized by the Mormons, whose eccentricities were condemned by many, even by Mark Twain. This sense for current topics must be attributed to Taylor's journalistic rather than to his literary sense. *The Prophet*, a realistic play not intended for the stage, suffered not only from dullness and irrelevance but also from Taylor's vagueness, which explains why many readers did not understand it.

XII Home Pastorals, Ballads and Lyrics (*1875*)[63]

Taylor had not published a collection of short poems since 1864, so *Home Pastorals* contained most of those published in periodicals during the previous ten years. The collection consists of three long poems in hexameters, with a proem and envoi dealing with the joys of rural life. The ballads continue the rural motif in four-line stanzas of fourteeners. The third section of the book contains twenty-five miscellaneous lyrics, while the fourth consists of three odes written for public occasions.

The book shows no marked advance over Taylor's previous lyrics; indeed, his few well-known poems are nearly all products of his early years. These later poems are less sensuous and diffuse, and more restrained than his earlier verse. It is noteworthy that he tried hexameters at this time, when Longfellow was also interested in them; but Taylor thought he had discovered the *real* hexameter. In a letter to Stedman, he said: "... The Germans *have* discovered the best hexameter. I can rapidly give you an idea of it;—*Four feet* dactylic, with an occasional trochee to vary the music. The fifth *inevitably* a dactyl. The sixth generally a trochee, but now and then a spondee, introduced when necessary to rest the ear. *No spondaic feet in the middle of the line.* This is the usual form, and it is very agreeable: -u/ -uu/ -uu/ -u/ -uu/ -u. Try a dozen lines, and I think you will be able to get the effect."[64]

In the Proem, Taylor announces that he is tired of foreign scenes; he intends, therefore, to "seek my songs in the quiet fields of my boyhood." In such a place, he says, if "song is . . . to be found, I must seek it within me." The first pastoral deals with his youth, his restlessness, and his desire to escape rural life. Yet after much travel he decided that the place to study man was at home:

Give me to know him, here, where inherited laws and disguises
Hide him at times from himself,—where his thought is chiefly collective,
Where, with numberless others fettered like slaves in a coffle,
Each insists he is free, inasmuch as his bondage is willing.

(St. V)

In the second pastoral, Taylor desires temporary release from literary activity and speculates on his career: "Idly balancing fortunes, feeling the spite of them, maybe,—/ For the little withheld outweighs the much that is given. . . ." Again, the sight of homes reminds him of his neighbors, who "Stand aghast at my dream of the sun, and the sound, and the splendor" (St. VII). Like most men, Taylor wanted to be understood; and, also like most men, he was never able to make others understand. He feels superior to the world in which he was born, but he needs reassurance that he did the right thing by taking the different and lonelier path.

In the third pastoral, he proceeds to a deeper questioning:

Where, when the wont is deranged, shall I find a permanent foothold?
Stripped of the rags of Time I see the form of my being,
Born of all that ever has been, and haughtily reaching
Forward to all that comes,—yet certain, this moment, of nothing.

(St. VI)

At this point, however, he hears a reassuring voice:

". . .Be calm, for to doubt is to seek whom
None can escape, and the soul is dulled with an idle acceptance.
. . . .
Over thy head, behold! the wing with its measureless shadow
Spread against the light, is the wing of the Angel of Unfaith,
Chosen of God to shield the eyes of men from his Glory."

(St. VIII)

Poetry

He concludes that out of some conception of "the nearness and farness of God" is born some hope and comfort. Though Taylor had abandoned the Quaker tendencies of his family, he was not irreligious; he held to some conception of a vague but Christian deity. His views were not radical, nor simpleminded. His optimism is like Browning's though perhaps more critical. Taylor is aware of new knowledge about the Bible and archeology, yet he clings to the idea of a supernatural agency, and of immortality.

In the Envoi, he says that in the country he has had peace: "Here, escaped from the conflict of taste, the confusion of voices/ Heard in a land where the form of Art abides as a stranger,/ Come to me definite hopes and clearer possible duties" (St. I). And he ends the poem with praise of his wife.

The home pastorals are among Taylor's best verse, despite the odd, jerky quality of the hexameters; for he describes with feeling and precision a life he knew well. The personal details are also important; for, like other Romantic poets, he wrote best about himself, or about things that touched his experience somewhere. It was in dealing with large themes that he lapsed into vagueness and platitudes.

The ballads have a similar interest; they are, however, less personal and more Quakerish. "The Quaker Widow," which some critics thought his best poem, is an interior monologue by an old woman who mourns the loss of her husband and the fact that her daughter is slipping away from Quaker practices. The poem is occasionally moving, but does not escape Genteel sentimentality:

It is not right to wish for death; the Lord disposes best.
His spirit comes to quiet hearts, and fits them for his rest;
And that He halved our little flock was merciful, I see:
For Benjamin has two in heaven, and two are left with me.
(St. XIV)

These poems show some imaginative insight into the minds and feelings of country people and are a feat of sorts. They are written in the language of the characters without quite being in dialect. They were popular; and, after Taylor's death, they were republished in a separate volume with elaborate sentimental illustrations.

The lyrics in this volume are not striking, and perhaps "Casa Guidi Windows" offers a fair sample. In eleven five-line stanzas, this poem recounts Taylor's recovery from a near-fatal illness in the house where Browning and his wife had lived. Taylor imagined that his life had been saved by the spirit of Elizabeth Barrett Browning:

> She came, whom Casa Guidi's chambers knew,
> And know more proudly, an Immortal, now;
> The air without a star was shivered through
> With the resistless radiance of her brow,
> And glimmering landscapes from the darkness grew.
> (St. V)

These lyrics are competent enough, and the volume displays his usual versatility. But the language is seldom memorable, and there is rarely a striking line or phrase, despite the great variety of form. What they lack is what Beatty called the "inevitability of great poetry."

Generally, "The Quaker Widow" was the most admired poem in this volume; for, according to Stedman, it was "unexcelled in truth and tenderness of feeling." The pastorals were good poems—simple, unpretentious, and genuine. The ballads are less remarkable but interesting. The volume illustrates, however, once more the discrepancy between Taylor's desires and talents; he had the perversity to want the wrong things and to subordinate his real talents. There may not have been much more he could say in these forms about the rural life in which he grew up, but he desired success with the more formal and conventional poetic forms in which he did least well.

XIII   The National Ode (1876)[65]

One form Taylor essayed with some frequency was the occasional poem. He wrote quite a number for all sorts of occasions, and he sometimes recited them. He did not admire the genre, but he was willing to practice it both for the money and for the opportunity to appear in public; for, a skilled lecturer, public appearances did not bother him. It would be difficult to list all the occasions for which he composed something, usually verse. He gave, as has been noted, the Phi Beta Kappa poem at Harvard in 1850 when he was only twenty-five. Later the same year, he read another poem at Columbia—nearly all of which he wrote the night before, "for I could not sooner bring my hand to touch the hated task. It was the most arduous piece of work I ever accomplished."[66] He even won a song-writing contest run by P. T. Barnum for Jenny Lind; but, since two of the three judges were his friends, this outcome was not surprising. On that occasion he remarked that his only inspiration "was the hope of getting the two hundred dollars."

In 1872, however, he resolved "never again to write . . . a poem for an occasion. I have resisted at least a hundred applications in the last fifteen years."[67] Despite this resolution, he was in 1875 writing an ode for the presentation of a bust of Goethe in Central Park. His great chance came when he was asked to write the National Ode for the centennial celebration of the United States on July 4, 1876. He was originally asked to write the hymn; but, when the ode commission was successively rejected by Bryant, Longfellow, Lowell, Whittier, and Holmes, the committee turned to Taylor. He knew this sequence of events, but he was not insulted. He worked hard and produced his best-known effort in the genre, *The National Ode.*

Indeed, Taylor's greatest fame with occasional poetry came from *The National Ode,* for its reception by the crowd was notable. According to his wife, his presence "stilled the noise and tumult of those before him, hushed even the lively creatures in the branches, and made the vast audience listen";[68] it was a "real victory for Poetry." When he finished, "a great shout rose"; Taylor was delighted to have "moved the common people." What moved "the people" is not difficult to see, for the poem (in eleven long stanzas) was patriotic, rhetorical, and rose to a crescendo of expression. It said that "Liberty's latest daughter" was in the sunrise of power while Asia drifted into the shadow and while Europe basked in the "ripened ray." When past powers ask what right America has to power, the answer is that it has created a nation out of virgin soil—a process described in detail. The nation has also combined the best of all races, though, "broad-based under all,/ Is planted England's oaken-hearted mood";

> To one strong race all races here unite:
> Tongues melt in hers, hereditary foemen

Forget their sword and slogan, kith and clan:
'T was glory, once, to be a Roman:
She makes it glory, now, to be a man!
(St. I-3)

Americans must strive to deserve power and the good opinion of
the world through work, knowledge, goodness, love, and art.

Taylor was pleased with the poem and its reception. He noted
"a dozen warmly appreciative newspaper notices, and three dis-
paraging sneers." He also received the usual congratulations
from Whittier and others; but later commentators thought less
of the poem. Stedman remarked sadly that "it was not the one
new, bold, original production, which ... becomes a lasting portion of national literature."[69] Smyth agreed that "few of the verses
cling, like Lowell's, to the memory." To Beatty, "Taylor was
simply out of his element. He could only write in vague, often
turgid and incoherent, language concerning our progress and
our forebears; he could only suggest, weakly, his far-from-weak
awareness of our significance in the world, the promise of our
future."[70] F. L. Pattee called the ode "one of the greatest failures
in the history of American literature."[71] These criticisms are
close to the truth; for the ode is vague, abstract, and bombastic.
Perhaps Taylor missed a great opportunity, or perhaps his language could not rise to fulfill the concepts of his imagination;
but, as his remarks on occasional poetry indicate, he did not
take such tasks very seriously.

The *Gettysburg Ode* is not bad. Faced with the problem of
outdoing Lincoln, whose address Taylor recognized as a great
work, he simply quoted from it in his first stanza. The poem, in
ten stanzas of unequal length, praises the dead, regrets their
death, and explains the values they died for:

We see the ghost of deeds they might have done,
The phantom homes that beaconed their endeavor;
The seeds of countless lives, in them begun,
That might have multiplied for us forever!
(St. V)

But pain and suffering were given "to teach us all the freeman's
sacred duty!" The dead are then compared with those of all past
battles in which courage and liberty were involved—

> They fought for a continent and made it secure.
>   From other basis never arose a nation!
> For strength is born of struggle, faith of doubt,
>   Of discord law, and freedom of oppression.
>
>   (St. IX)

The loss of these men is great; but theirs is the price men must pay for liberty. There is no original thought in this ode; but the occasion probably forbade it. Moreover, the poem expresses what everyone expected; the sentiments are standard but not, therefore, untrue.

Taylor's views on occasional poetry appear in his advice to Sidney Lanier, for whom he helped secure the task of writing the cantata for the centennial. "'Occasional' poetical work should always be brief, appropriate in idea, and technically good," Taylor said. "One dare not be imaginative or particularly original."[72] There is some truth in this statement, though it grows partly from Taylor's contempt for the public. It is also true that none of his public poems are original or imaginative.

XIV Prince Deukalion (*1878*)[73]

Taylor's last volume, *Prince Deukalion,* was a verse drama in four acts in which the leading characters speak in blank verse most of the time; but many songs are interspersed, the other characters speak in other meters, and the result is a remarkable collection of metrical and stanza forms, a *tour de force* exhibiting Taylor's poetic skill. The characters are abstractions, and the time covered is two thousand years. There is, therefore, a great deal of murky symbolism; in fact, Taylor had to add a prose argument to explain what was happening in the poem. He asserts that the aim of the poem is "to picture forth the struggle of Man . . . to reach the highest, justest, happiest, hence most perfect condition of Human life on this planet," a condition hampered by such forces as knowledge, religion, political organization, art, and animal nature. In other words, progress, fitful as it may be, is the subject of the poem.

The leading characters (or abstractions) are Prince Deukalion and Pyrrha, who represent "Ideals of possible Manhood and possible Womanhood, decreed from the first, not yet incarnate, nor permitted to celebrate their high nuptials until both shall

be fulfilled in Human Life." The first act concerns the "passing
away of the Classic Faith, and the emergence of Christianity
from its hidden places of abode, to the daylight of acceptance."
The change seems not exactly desirable; for Gaea, the Earth
spirit, worries about her children who have changed so radically.
But, when Eros appears, Gaea rejoices that at least Love remains
with Man.

Deukalion and Pyrrha visit his father Prometheus in Hades,
and he promises to return to earth sometime:

> . . .I set in Man
> Immortal seeds of pure activities,
> By mine atonement freed, to burst and bloom
> In distant, proud fulfillment.
>
> (p. 42)

Eos, goddess of Dawn, confirms that a better time is coming
"when the race/ Lifts unto me a fixed, believing face,/ I will
return!" Deukalion is to be the vehicle of this progress.

The second act occurs a thousand years later when life is
dominated by the Catholic Church which is represented in the
poem by Medusa. She is "no figure of the Faith of her day and
world, but only of that Ecclesiastical System which essayed to
shape and compel to its service all the forces of life." Deukalion
is repelled by Christian shrines which blend torture with distor-
tion. Yet, when two shepherds worship the Virgin and saints, he
sees that "In these new names extinguished miracles/ Sweetly
renew themselves. . . ." But he also accuses Medusa of using
faith to control men. Pyrrha adds that Medusa's secret is sex:
"Sexless thyself, the secret of the sex/ Is lightly caught by
thee. . . ." When faced with Urania (Science), Medusa quivers;
presumably Urania will be the agency of her demise.

The third act is by far the murkiest. The time is the nineteenth century and, according to Taylor, "another Faith, where-
of Calchas, High-Priest, represents the inflexible, despotic The-
ology, hath supplanted Medusa in the Lands of the North."
Though the Catholic Church lost much power, Taylor saw a new
threat from Protestantism. Deukalion attacks Calchas as he did
Medusa, demanding greater freedom for man:

...Give knowledge room,
Yea, room to doubt, and sharp denial's gust
That makes all things unstable! Tremble not
When stern Urania writes the words of Law:
Make once more Life the noble thing it was
When Gods were human, or the nobler thing
It shall be when The God becomes divine!
(p. 114)

This section seems to allude to the evolution controversy, when Protestantism, at first a liberator from Rome, became itself a vested interest that attacked the new scientific knowledge. Urania, on the other hand, represents the arrogance of science: "Past? I know no Past! . . . Nothing is, save Law."

In the fourth and final act, Taylor "adventureth only far enough into the Future to predict the beginning of an Era." Yet the reader finds everywhere in the drama "the declaration of Growth, Immortality, God." Much of this message appears in a debate between Agathon (who speaks for Taylor) and Urania. When Agathon denies death (affirms immortality), Urania asks, "why, to flatter life, wilt thou repeat/ The unproven solace?" Agathon replies:

Proven by its need!—
By fates so large no fortune can fulfill;
By wrong no earthly justice can atone;
By promises of love that keep love pure;
And all rich instincts, powerless of aim,
Save chance, and time, and aspiration wed
To freer forces, follow! By the trust
Of the chilled Good that at life's very end
Puts forth a root and feels its blossom sure!
Yea, by thy law!—since every being holds
Its final purpose in the primal cell,
And here the radiant destiny o'erflows
Its visible bounds, enlarges what it took
From sources past discovery, and predicts
No end, or, if an end, the end of all!
(pp. 143-44)

Prometheus summons Buddha, Medusa, Calchas, and Urania to present their views. When Buddha, for example, counsels renunciation, Agathon replies:

But I accept,—even all this conscious life
Gives in its fullest measure,—gladness, health,
Clean appetite, and wholeness of my claim
To knowledge, beauty, aspiration, power!
Joy follows action, here; and action bliss,
Hereafter!

(pp. 150-51)

Urania mocks man's desire to feel "a human heart-beat somewhere in the void,/ And rescue their imagined essences,/ Distinct and conscious, from eternal dust!" Agathon answers that
"Men grow,/ But not beyond their hearts,—possess, enjoy,/ Yet,
being dependent, ever must believe...." The final statement of
the poem is made by Prometheus:

For Life, whose course not here began,
Must fill the utmost sphere of Man,
And, so expanding, lifted be
Along the line of God's decree,
To find in endless growth all good,—
In endless toil, beatitude.
Seek not to know him; yet aspire
As atoms toward the central fire!

(p. 171)

This poem contains some of Taylor's best verse though, as a
whole, it is uneven. Its quality derives partly from the fact
that he seriously feels what he is saying. To Taylor, a belief in
immortality was real; and his argument is related to his own
situation: the fact that nothing in life is completed argues a
world where completion may become reality. Perhaps he thinks
of a world where his own work may be completed—where
he can devote himself to embodying his own most idealistic
conceptions.

Still, the poem also embodies some of Taylor's chief faults—
for example, his devotion to the abstract and the ideal. He seemed
unable to concretize his conceptions. To embody an idea in such
a manner that it is both a symbol and a reality seemed foreign
to him; his only way of handling abstractions is abstractly. For
instance, Medusa represents the Catholic Church; but Medusa
is itself an abstract conception, and thus one abstract idea per-
sonifies another. Even Goethe concretized in a way that Taylor

never does: Faust is mankind, but he is also Johannes Faust; Marguerite is love, but she is also a real woman. Despite Taylor's admiration for Goethe, he never seemed to grasp this method. Though *Prince Deukalion* challenges comparison with *Faust*, is intended as a Goethean poem, and deals with similar themes, it works so abstractly as to make its best points ineffective. The result is that the play has little human interest, for it deals only with ideas.

Taylor's devotion to Classical materials is also tiring. These subjects were alive during the flood of the Romantic period, but to have shepherds and nymphs prancing around in 1878 seems ridiculous. It shows that, while Taylor was aware of the intellectual currents of his era, he was less interested in the actual day-to-day life of it. To worry about the qualities of perfect manhood and womanhood in a distant era seems a strange escapism, and then to complain about a lack of readers seems a kind of perversity. "Probably," said Smyth, "not many of those who essayed 'Prince Deukalion' held on to the close of the first act."[74] One could hardly disagree.

Prince Deukalion was Taylor's last published work, and it is something of a summary of his beliefs. He believed in progress, and that men and women, as well as society, were moving toward perfection; he believed in immortality, in some kind of existence after death, in a God of some kind, one never precisely described. While Taylor accepted Christian principles, he anticipated something beyond Christianity, and greater. These beliefs are not, of course, unusual or remarkable.

Many critics thought this poem Taylor's best work, and he certainly had poured more of himself into it than into any previous work. Beatty, who usually had a low opinion of Taylor's poetry, thought this poem his "wisest and most important. For once he has content to sustain him. He has something of high significance to say, and he says it well."[75] Stedman thought it "admirable for richness and variety of measures"; for, to Taylor, the "progress of mankind" was one of the "most elevating" of poetic themes. Of course, Longfellow told Taylor it was "one of the grandest conceptions in literature"; and Whittier called it "a great poem," one recalling "the grand dramas of the immortal Greeks."[76] However, the poem was called "Faustian" by many reviewers, although Krumpelmann makes a good case for the view that it is closest, not to *Faust*, but to Goethe's unfinished *Pandora*; and he devotes some space to detailing similarities, making clear that Taylor was unusually dependent on his German sources.[77]

It is difficult, perhaps ungracious, to say that a poet's most serious work is a failure, and that is not entirely true of the poem. But the remarks just quoted about its subject matter, statement, relevance, and verse still stand. Probably, it is Taylor's best poem; but, whereas Thorp says it gives evidence of a new maturity,[78] the poem seems rather a fitting end, a culmination of the best that he was capable of thinking and doing. Taylor referred to it as "the poem of my life," and his wife said it "contains the sum of his ripest views of life and the world." That the poem contained his most serious belief cannot be doubted; for, as Taylor wrote to Paul Hamilton Hayne:

> . . .The very wisdom and wonder of the universe and its law prove conclusively to me that the intuitions of power and knowledge in ourselves, which we cannot fulfill here, *assure us* of continued being. If those laws are good,—as we see they are,—then what is ordered for us is also good. . . .*True* harmony between natures in this life certainly predicts continuance in the next; but how or in what manner it shall be continued is beyond us, and I have not felt the least fear. . . .I *know* (but I cannot demonstrate) that my being cannot be annihilated. . . .[79]

Perhaps it would be cruel to analyze too closely a work that grows out of such fervent conviction. *Prince Deukalion* is in many ways a good poem. If it is dull, if it deals with questions with which readers no longer concern themselves, if its faith seems naïve and blind to modern readers, perhaps the fault is the readers' more than Taylor's.

XV   *Collected Works*[80]

The Poetical Works of Bayard Taylor (1880) and *The Dramatic Works of Bayard Taylor* (1880) appeared two years after Taylor's death; the first was edited by George Boker; the second, by Taylor's wife, Marie Hansen-Taylor. They remain the standard edition, for Taylor has not been the subject of much scholarship or criticism since the turn of the twentieth century. A few later collections were made, but they were drawn from this Household Edition of 1880, which Boker alleged contained "the entire poetical works" of Taylor. Although Boker also claimed to have added a number of poems never before published, he followed largely the sequence and headings of the earlier edition of 1864; by and large, he simply added to it the contents of subsequent volumes. However, Boker did not include a considerable number of Taylor's poems. From the 1864 collection (roughly half of this volume), he dropped forty-one poems, but he added five; he also included many poems that were not in the original publications. The result, therefore, is not "complete," though it is the most nearly complete edition that exists.

Although Boker's preface is appreciative, he hedges about the quality of the verse. He says Taylor "believed himself to be a poet,—of what stature and quality it is now for the world to decide,—and in that faith he wrought at his vocation with an assiduity . . . that was wonderful as an exhibition of human industry."[81] But Boker adds that, to Taylor, "poetry was a second religion, or an intellectual continuation of that natural, moral sentiment which lifts man above himself and his fortunes in his aspiration after immortality and supernal life."[82] Generally, the preface is praise which, while genuine, is neither excessive nor flattering.

XV *Assessment of the Poetry*

It should be clear from this account that Taylor was not a first-class poet. Despite his many volumes of verse, his "The Bedouin Song" is the only poem that came near to being a part of the general imagination; and even that is no longer true. There is no poem of his that forms part of the literary imagination anywhere. If persons who study literature know little of his verse, then it is reasonable to say that it is pretty dead.

When reading the entire work of such a poet, one finds that sometimes it isn't bad. Usually, it is technically competent and various in subject and form. Occasionally there are felicitous lines or nice phrases. Yet, the poetry doesn't stick in the mind; as one of his friends once said, it seems "made"; it is essentially vacuous. Yeats once said rhetoric was the will doing the work of the imagination, and this statement may be one way of explaining the defects of such poetry. Taylor was certainly long on will and desire, but his talent was perhaps not large enough for lasting poetry, or was of a different kind.

For Taylor, however, there was another factor at work. While he liked poetry and believed in its efficacy and force, it also had for him a personal social significance. That is, while he wrote prose for money, he wrote poetry for respectability, as any number of his remarks indicate. In his day, poetry was still highly respected (and the view of the poet as seer and moralist was current); the immense popularity of Longfellow and Tennyson shows how widely admired poets were. As a poor boy, Taylor envied that kind of success; and he saw poetry as, among other things, a means to social respectability. His many visits to the New England Genteel poets showed him an ideal of life which he thought desirable—casual, comfortable, intellectual; and this view was reinforced by his visits to the homes of English poets. The Genteel tradition, in this sense, furnished Taylor with his fundamental ideals about a way of life to which he might aspire.

But the kind of poetry the Genteel tradition produced was consistent with the pleasant lives such poets lived—cheery, comfortable, sentimental. There is little that is disturbing in Longfellow's verse; the same is true of Taylor's. Their poetry emphasized musical quality and "story"; it appealed in subject to a largely uncritical audience of women; and its technical competence satisfied other kindred poets. The limitations this audience placed on poetry were great, and the result was abstractness, "tone and mood" creation—a kind of skillful vacuity. Taylor could write this sort of thing reasonably well. His most original work was *Poems of the Orient,* not a bad volume in many ways—lyrical, colorful, sensuous, exotic. But, like all of his poetry, it reminds one of someone else's poetry—in this case, of Moore's *Hebrew Melodies* and of Byron's exotic romances—*Lara, The Giaour.* Perhaps by the time Taylor reached *Prince Deukalion,* after his careful work on *Faust,* he had some idea of what poetry should be; and it is possible that *Prince Deukalion* suggests a new maturity.

But in modern terms, Taylor's verse was not very good. Those who appreciate the economy, precision, and intellectuality of modern verse will dismiss Taylor's as trivial, vague, and profuse—though many of his contemporaries admired it. One is forced to consider the possibility that in his own day he had a somewhat inflated reputation. But this, too, was part of the Genteel tradition. For the careful nurture of his own reputation, and the attention he gave to his friends, and they gave to him, the conscious manipulation of the literary world—all these things help explain why Taylor was more famous then than now —as well as why his reputation declined so rapidly when neither he nor his friends were alive to keep it living. Taylor wanted to be a poet so much that his desire is almost painful to read about. He worked at his art with a wonderful patience and assiduity. But his career demonstrates, if it demonstrates anything, that poets are not made but born.

CHAPTER *5*

Critical and Other Works

I *Translations*

THE *Faust* translation is Taylor's most important work, and his only book which has survived. Still considered standard in some quarters, it is currently available in the Modern Library and in the Oxford World's Classics. Taylor seriously aimed at making it the standard version; indeed, he said that it was going to be "the" English *Faust* and that no one need translate it again after him. He compared all existing translations, mastered the scholarship (extensive even then), and studied the history of the Faust legend; he did all that sheer labor could do to contribute to a fine translation. In the process, he became an expert on Goethe, on *Faust*, and on some areas of German literature. And he did all this work in the midst of fulfilling other duties, for *Faust* did not bring in any money.

The origin of his interest in things German has already been suggested. His marriage to Marie Hansen was important; it is perhaps significant that her wedding gift to him was a copy of *Faust*. Of course, the influence of German culture, at this time, in America was beginning to be extensive—an influence to which Taylor was to contribute. Taylor's interest was probably stimulated also by the possibility of selling his own books in Germany. His wife translated many of them, and he did much to encourage the growth of his reputation there not only as an intermediary between Germany and America but also as a significant American literary figure. Even today, Taylor is probably better known in Germany than in the United States.

Taylor, however, did not actually do much translating. Over the years, he translated a number of lyrics or fragments of longer poems; but, except for *Faust*, he never undertook a complete

156

work, with the possible exception of Friedrich von Schiller's *Don Carlos,* which he adapted for Lawrence Barrett in 1878. Apparently, Taylor wanted to be known as an American poet who, like Longfellow and Irving, had translated a great work to show his knowledge and skill; but he did not want to be a professional translator.

Taylor said he had started *Faust* twenty years before it was published. He did translate some passages in the early 1850's, but the translation as it exists was the work of the last six or seven years before its appearance in 1871; and the great bulk of it was done intensively during the last three years. The first part of *Faust* was published in December, 1870 (dated 1871); the second part, the following March.[1] Its format was uniform with Longfellow's Dante and with Bryant's Homer, making the work seem part of a great series of American translations and implying Taylor's equality with the great American poets of the day. This impression was reinforced by the treatment accorded him by his shrewd publisher, Fields, who gave a dinner to which were invited all the New England worthies whom Taylor had so assiduously cultivated. Sitting around a bust of Goethe were Longfellow, Lowell, Holmes, Howells, Aldrich, and Osgood; Whittier and Emerson, unable to come, sent regrets and compliments.[2] Such recognition, said Taylor's wife, went straight to his heart; "for he loved his work, he loved poetry and all art with a passion. . . ."[3] Later, he wrote proudly to his mother about his "glorious visit to Boston, and dinner with the authors. 'Faust' is everywhere pronounced a great success and will give me a permanent place in our literature."[4]

However much Taylor enjoyed the praise and recognition of his fellows, he did not intend to neglect promoting his work. He was a shrewd man; his frequent advice to Fields about format and price and about the number of copies to print, to give away, and to whom indicate he was vitally concerned with sales; though he insisted to friends that *Faust* couldn't sell, he did as much as an author can to ensure its success. To Fields, he wrote:

If my "Faust" is what I mean it to be, it will have a permanent place in translated literature. No one is likely, very soon, to undertake an equal labor. An immediate success will be much more important to me than that of any work I have yet published. . . .I think the aspects are good just now. The German ascendency in Europe, Marie Seebach's acting here, and various similar influences, may all be so many indirect helps. I beg you, therefore, to take all usual measures to set the work fairly afloat, and catch up every little side-wind that may be turned towards its sails.[5]

Apparently, his care worked. Reviews were nearly unanimously favorable, but much of this response was probably due to a careful selection of reviewers. Krumpelmann reports that, of forty-seven reviews he examined, forty-five were favorable; one, middling; one, unfavorable.[6] Even if book reviewing in America at the time was rather corrupt (and Fields exerted influence in many journals), forty-five of forty-seven remains a little short of amazing.

The picture is somewhat blurred, however, by a copy of a suppressed review owned by the Harvard Library, which was to have been printed in the April, 1872, issue of the *North American Review*. The following note in longhand, signed by Henry Adams, is appended: "This notice, written originally by a strong admirer of Mr. Taylor, but much changed by me in tone, led to a protest from the author, and a request from Mr. Osgood that the notice should be suppressed. Which was done."[7] Since the review is not really unfavorable, it is difficult to see what Taylor objected to—probably to the fact that it was a twenty-five page article which Adams had cut to a ten-page review. The reviewer does say that translating in the original meters "is a devotion to principle which approaches fanaticism," complains that the work is "somewhat pedantic," and criticizes some inaccuracies; but he also calls it "a great achievement in this kind of translation."

What is disturbing is that Taylor was able to suppress the review and that he desired to do so. How many other reviews Taylor or his publisher was able to suppress is not known, but such an episode leaves in doubt the value of reviews as a guide to the book's reception; however, it must be remembered that the *North American Review* was owned at this time by Fields's publishing house. Taylor was outraged; and he complained that the "course of the N.A.R. has been excessively clannish and narrow" by favoring New England authors over others. "If there is to be an exclusive Boston circle created in our literature," he said, "the sooner the rest of us know it the better."[9] He soon apologized, but he added that the *Review* "should have been prompt to notice, however briefly, the appearance of a work which has more than a personal character,—which is accepted, both in England and Germany, as one of the indications of our American culture. I think this ought to be done, independently of residence, and personal relations with the editor."[10] One can sympathize with Taylor's feelings, for Adams's snobbishness is well known, as was the tendency for New England writers to become ingrown. Yet Taylor's just complaint is somewhat vitiated by his own willingness to suppress a not too unfavorable review.

As to how good Taylor's translation of *Faust* is, the view that it was the best was widely accepted for a long time. Contemporary critics were strongly in its favor; so were German critics; but subsequent critics have raised doubts. One of the first to shatter this unanimity of opinion was Juliana Haskell, who, in a Columbia dissertation in 1908, attacked it vigorously.[11] But before noticing the basis of Miss Haskell's attacks, one should review some of Taylor's principles which he applied in his translation.

First, it should be noted that Taylor had a theory of translation, the first principle of which was that the translator should efface himself. Second, he argued that poetry should be translated in the same meters if possible, and it was possible with *Faust* because of similarities between the English and German languages—though he did not mean "a rigid, unyielding adherence to every foot, line, and rhyme . . . although this has very nearly been accomplished."[12] He was proud of his success in putting the poem into the original meters; but he has been accused of a mindless adherence to form, of a belief that form equals content, and of indulgence in padding, inaccuracy, and unnatural English.

Third, Taylor insisted that only a poet could translate another poet. He said the translator "must feel, and be guided by, a secondary inspiration. Surrendering himself to the full possession of the spirit which shall speak through him, he receives, also, a portion of the same creative power."[13] Finally, he made some odd remarks about English; for example, that English meter "compels the use of inversions" and "admits many verbal liberties prohibited to prose." But, as Beatty has pointed out, inversions

have not been much used in English since the eighteenth century;
and why Taylor thought they had been is somewhat puzzling.
It should be noted, though, that his own poetry is full of inversions, so there was evidently some defect in his knowledge.

Miss Haskell's attack centered on these very points. Taylor
claimed literalness; she lists (tiresomely) places where he de-
parted from the sense, padded lines, distorted meaning, and even
changed the meter. "He found himself unable at times to apply
his theory," she says; "on the other hand he applied his theory,
transferred the form and somehow the poetry was not transferred with it."[14] To his argument that only a poet can translate
another poet, she replied that Taylor was not a very good poet.
She complained that he had Latinized Goethe; and, if this effect is unavoidable in English, then it denies his belief that the
languages are similar. She quoted Barrett Wendell's remark that
Taylor's *Faust* "in nowise resembles normal English," and she
concluded that "Bayard Taylor had the intelligence of a well-
trained journalist; he had not the emotions or the nice discrimina-
tion of a poet."[15] Concluding that Taylor's *Faust* is neither English nor Goethe, she holds that it is "an inadequate translation."

It has been alleged that this assault on Taylor's most famous
work resulted in his widow's giving his papers to Cornell University rather than to Columbia.[16] Yet much of what Haskell says
is obviously true, though her conclusion is not necessarily correct. The translation is frequently not good English; but it is,
at times, very successful; and translating it in the original meters,
while sometimes unnatural, was a *tour de force* which communi-
cates something of the variety and vigor of the poem. Thorp
argues that, despite its faults, the translation supplies the English
reader with as much Goethe as he is likely to get.[17] Beatty agrees
that it is "one of the best in English," and that leaning on Goethe
supplied Taylor with a depth that was foreign to him.[18]

Krumpelmann objects that Haskell's criticism is largely struc-
tural and linguistic; that most of the faults she notes would not
be noted by Germans; and that most of the "irregularities"
are due "not to a conscious or unconscious imitation of the German order, but to the fact that finding that certain transposi-
tions and the like facilitated his imitation of the form . . . he
availed himself of these liberties. . . ."[19] Moreover, subsequent

translators have leaned on Taylor, he says, and have been influenced by him "even down into the twentieth century."[20]

When *Faust* appeared, Taylor's translation was the most complete ever produced; he "succeeded as well as any translator, and better than any of his predecessors, in remaining faithful to the sense of the original," and in "preserving the music, rhythm and *Stimmung* of the German poem."[21] And his Notes, while to some extent antiquated, are still "not only interesting and instructive, but also essential." It should also be noted that Taylor was the first to translate the complete second part and to defend it as an integral part of the whole poem.

Obviously, there are many things about Taylor's *Faust* that are unsatisfactory and which one may find detailed in such criticism as that of Haskell. But, despite these flaws, critics of the twentieth century think the book has great value; and it is still one of the best translations available. Certainly, *Faust* is Taylor's one enduring work; it gave him the place in American literature that he so ardently sought; it became a standard. The fate of his own poetry would be disappointing to him, but he would probably be pleased with the reputation of his *Faust*.

Taylor's notes to *Faust* (1870), might well be included under "criticism." They are so extensive as to constitute a good-sized volume; with Prefaces and Appendices, they total some three hundred and fifteen pages of fine print. It is unfortunate that available reprints of Taylor's *Faust* do not include the notes, for they are quite valuable and show that Taylor was indeed an expert on this work. He had mastered the scholarship, consulted original manuscripts, knew all the translations that had been made, and for years debated fine points with friends and strangers. The result is that the Notes, as of 1870, constitute the most thorough summary of scholarship available—all of which, he said, "led me back to find in the author of *Faust* his own best commentator."

Sometimes the notes explicate, or give a brief biography of some person mentioned in the text, or quote parallel passages; sometimes they contain information about Goethe himself, explain his ideas or intentions, give alternative translations, or quote from other translations; and the appendices contain a history of the Faust legend. In sum, they constitute an extended commentary on *Faust*; marked by intelligence, taste, and interpretive ability, they are one of Taylor's most impressive achievements.

In the light of *Faust*, Taylor's other translations are not very important. He translated lyrics occasionally—eighty-six poems or portions of poems, according to Krumpelmann, from 1850 to 1877;[22] and the poets he was most attracted to were F. Freiligrath, Johann Uhlan, Schiller, Goethe, Heinrich Heine, Joseph von Eichendorff, and Friedrich Ruckert. (See p. 220) He was once commissioned by the actor Lawrence Barrett to translate and adapt Schiller's *Don Carlos* for the stage. But, since the official biography barely mentions this work, not much is known about it. It was neither acted nor published, and it seems to have been lost for some time. However, a scholar who saw Taylor's manuscript described it as containing roughly half the original, and he thought it might be actable; but this is pure speculation.[23]

II   *Parodies*

That Taylor had a satirical streak can be seen in his novels and frequently in his letters. Though his poetry is serious, he had a good sense of humor. *The Echo Club and Other Literary Diversions* (1876)[24] is a group of parodies of contemporary poets, which originated (according to his wife) during his early life in New York when he and friends gathered for an evening's entertainment of poetic contests. In 1871, Taylor "conceived the notion of giving a certain body to the fun. He was half vexed, half entertained at the sudden rise in America of the dialect school of poetry," and he fancied that he "could make his parodies not only bits of fun, but sly criticisms as well."[25]

This idea, however, resulted in one of his many quarrels with Stoddard; for it was he who originally suggested collecting these pieces "as the work of a new poet." When Taylor used the material himself (dropping the "new poet" idea), Stoddard was miffed.[26] Of course, the minds of these men ran in the same channels so much of the time that it would not be accurate to say that Taylor borrowed the idea, for he might well have conceived it simultaneously. At any rate, the parodies were published as articles in the *Atlantic Monthly* over a period of eight months in 1872; and they appeared as a book four years later.

The material is arranged in eight "nights" during which sev-

eral poets gather in a beer cellar; each takes from a hat the name
of a contemporary whom he then proceeds to parody. Usually
there are four each night, but a few "extras" are added from time
to time. The four parodists supposedly have different viewpoints:
the Ancient is "the calmer judicial temper, in literary matters,
which comes from age and liberal study"; Zoilus, the "carping,
cynical, unconsciously arrogant critic"; Galahad, the "young,
sensational, impressive element in the reading public"; and the
Gannet "represents brilliancy without literary principle, the love
of technical effect, regardless of the intellectual conception of
a work" (viii-ix). In fact, however, it is not easy to distinguish
these differences; and the dominant voice is that of the Ancient,
whose views seem to be Taylor's.

On the first night, the poets parodied are Morris, Poe, and
Browning, the last one four different times. It should be mentioned that the Ancient defines parody as "a close imitation of
some particular poem" characteristic of an author; but he also
argues that something better would be to echo the author's
tone and manner. Most of Taylor's parodies, however, are tied to
specific poems of an author.

After the parodies, the Ancient comments on Poe's poetry; it
"has a hectic flush, a strange, fascinating, narcotic quality. . . ."
He adds that "there were two men in him: one, a refined gentleman, an aspiring soul, an artist among those who had little sense
of literary art; the other . . . 'Built his nest with the birds of
night.'" Browning, on the other hand, has a "wilfully artificial"
manner. "Sordello" is "perplexity, not profundity"; but Browning has a "royal brain, and we owe him too much to bear malice
against him."

The subjects of the parodies of the second night are an odd
lot: Keats, Emerson, Swinburne, Mrs. Sigourney, and E. C.
Stedman. These are prefaced by an argument from the Ancient
defending the practice of deferring to English criticism. American critics are too partisan and prejudiced, he says; indeed,
the lack of serious criticism is a familiar complaint of Taylor's.
The Keats parody, "Ode on a Jar of Pickles," while not bad,
convinces the critics that they should stay with the poets of their
own time. The Ancient's remarks on Swinburne are that he has
no equal as a "purely rhythmical genius" but that one should
wait for his ferment to settle; sensationalism means little in

poetry. In an interesting defense of Emerson, the critic asserts that "barring a few idiosyncrasies of expression," there are few authors so clear as Emerson.

The third night covers Thomas Holley Chivers, Barry Cornwall, Whittier, D. G. Rossetti, and T. B. Aldrich. The Ancient complains that the chief fault of popular authors is "intensity of epithet," or striving for attention by odd diction, a habit not conducive to permanence. "There are eternal laws of Art, to which the moral and spiritual aspirations of the author, which are generally relative to his own or the preceding age, must conform, if they would become eternal."

The parody of Whittier is not only extremely mild but is embedded in praise. According to the Ancient, Whittier "deserves all the love and reverence" one can give him; his poetic art "has refined and harmonized the moral quality . . . which . . . made his poetry seem partisan." The alloy has been melted out "in the pure and steady flame of his intellect." The Gannett, who writes the parody, offers to go to Massachusetts to show the poet what he has done for his approval.

Bryant is parodied on the fourth night; his prominent characteristics "are all so evenly and exquisitely blended in his verse, that no single one seems salient enough to take hold of." Holmes is described as having brought the "playful element" to American literature. "O, how tired I am of hearing that every poem should 'convey a lesson. . . .' Why, half our self-elected critics seem to be blind to the purely aesthetic character of our art!"—this is the Ancient's outburst. The last poet discussed, Tennyson, causes a good deal of comment. "I yield to no one in the profoundest respect for his noble loyalty to his art," says the Ancient; Tennyson has understood the nature of his gift, and he has spent his energies perfecting it.

The following night the discussion of Tennyson continues; and he is absolved of all blame for the crimes of his imitators. Poets parodied this night are Henry Tuckerman, Longfellow, Howells, Stoddard, and Mrs. Stoddard. Naturally, Longfellow gets most of the space; and, like Whittier, he is very gently handled. He has "advanced the front rank of our culture," says the Ancient, who praises his "purity, his refinement, and his constant reference to an ideal of life which so many might otherwise forget." As a crude nation, the United States needs his "sweet and clear and steady" influence.

On the sixth night, which begins with complaints about American reviewing and criticism, the Ancient assures all that good work will ultimately triumph over pettiness. He adds that the best critics are Lowell, E. P. Whipple, and George Ripley. The poets parodied are Lowell, Taylor himself, Elizabeth Browning, and George Boker. Naturally, the Ancient has a hard time with Lowell since he likes him so much, but he manages to produce "The Saga of Ahab Doolittle." About the only critical remark he can manage is that Lowell's poetry is "over-weighted with ideas." Taylor's remarks about himself are not unexpected. He parodies one of his early Oriental poems, and the comments are that he hasn't any definite place yet; he has too many irons in the fire; his tendency to rhetoric is his chief weakness; and signs of a new form of development appear in his recent poetry. These clearly represent Taylor's idea of his own chief faults.

The topic of discussion on the seventh night is whether America is suffering a period of decline in literature, or is on the verge of a new outburst of genius. The Gannet argues for the renaissance, but the Ancient thinks a great era has just passed. Poets parodied this night are perfectly absurd subjects: Jean Ingelow, James B. Read, Julia Ward Howe, Mr. and Mrs. Piatt, and William Winter, all of whom seem to be a waste of time; perhaps Taylor deliberately chose them to support the view of the Ancient. Discussion rambles on about the need of American poets to forego metrical correctness in favor of developing an individual style. Bayard Taylor is complimented incidentally by the Ancient for seeking "the substance of poetry, rather than the flash and glitter of its rhetorical drapery."

The last night begins with a discussion of the relationship between quality and popularity; and, to the Ancient, the "genuine poet is always the best judge of his own works, simply because he has an ideal standard by which he measures whatever he does"—a favorite view of Taylor's. The poets parodied are the "dialect" group: Whitman, Bret Harte, John Hay, and Joaquin Miller. The Ancient suggests that the popularity of such poets in England is explained by the conventional nature of poetry there and by the subsequent desire for anything new and racy. Zoilus concedes that in Whitman "there are splendid lines and brief passages . . . there is a modern, half-Bowery-boy, half-Emersonian apprehension of the old Greek idea of physical life. . . ." Indeed, the elements of a fine poet exist in Whitman but "in a state of chaos." The Ancient replies: "The same art which he despises would have increased his power and influence. He forgets that the poet must not only have somewhat to say, but must strenuously acquire the power of saying it most purely and completely. A truer sense of art would have prevented that fault which has been called immorality, but is only a coarse, offensive frankness" (155).

The Echo Club is an interesting book for those who enjoy parodies, for many of them are quite well done. The faults of the volume, however, are several: first, some of the parodies are so mild as to be ineffective; and they are so because Taylor wanted to avoid offending people like the New England worthies. Second, the prose setting was not a good idea, chiefly because Taylor's opinions are not remarkably perceptive. Third, at least half the parodies are of poets who are now so dead that most readers have never heard of them. And, of course, Taylor, in his usual fashion, managed to get his friends into the book as a form of publicity—Mr. and Mrs. Stoddard, Stedman, Boker, and Aldrich, not to mention himself.

Unfortunately, the book did not draw much attention. Taylor reported from Rome in 1873 that the original articles were creating a stir among American painters there; and he quotes Browning, who had told a friend they were the best parodies he had ever seen.[27] But the book itself fell dead from the press in 1876. Beatty thought *The Echo Club* marked by an "irritating timidity." This is quite true; but the parodies are good when Taylor did not know the writers personally, or when he cared little about their opinion. Beatty also thought Taylor's literary opinions here were important, but their significance is less certain. It is nice to know that the permanent in art is worth striving for and that temporary fame is not the same; that the sensuous and sensational are not the best features of poetry; that simplicity is a virtue; that technical skill is important but not all-important; that American criticism was bad, and English better; that preaching in poetry is not a good thing; and that a poet is the best judge of his own work. But none of these views is either profound or surprising.

Professor Trent, in his history of American literature, said it was pathetic to find Taylor publishing parodies on popular poets.[28] On the other hand, W. D. Howells thought they were "the best parodies ever written."[29] One of the strongest supporters of *The Echo Club*, oddly enough, was Juliana Haskell, who argued that the book was "a classic of its kind," as good as the Bab Ballads, or Edward Lear, or Lewis Carroll, and certainly "the best of the works of Bayard Taylor."[30] This praise is rather high; but *The Echo Club* is surely *one* of his best works. It is significant that Dwight MacDonald, in his recent collection of parodies (1960), included three from *The Echo Club*—on Poe, Browning, and Whitman.

III   *Studies in German Literature*

As has been noted, Taylor achieved some status as a translator of *Faust*, and as an intermediary between Germany and America; he probably achieved a somewhat exaggerated reputation in Germany. The same may be true, to a lesser degree, of his friends, whose work he "puffed" in Germany—Stoddard, Stedman, Boker, and Aldrich. Taylor was also helped by the political influence exerted in America by German-Americans; therefore, when he was appointed ambassador to Germany, he had the solid support of the German-American community.

Outside of a few biographies, there is very little criticism or explication of Taylor's work. His poetry, fiction, and criticism have been largely ignored by modern critics and scholars, who seem to feel that he was not an important poet. His German work, however, has been the subject of considerable criticism, mainly concerned with the translations and the German elements in his work.

On result of his reputation as a Germanist was his appointment as a nonresident professor of German literature at Cornell University in 1869, a post that demanded he give a series of lectures but not regularly. Thus, in 1870, he gave the first six lectures on Lessing, Klopstock, Schiller, Goethe, and Humboldt. In 1871, he read a new series on early German literature. In 1875, he delivered lectures on Lessing, Klopstock, Herder, Wieland, Richter, Schiller, and Goethe, while in 1877 he repeated those on early German literature. He also used these lectures elsewhere—

in 1876, at the Peabody Institute in Baltimore; in 1877, in New York City and Brooklyn; and, in 1877, at the Lowell Institute in Boston he gave the whole series of twelve. He also gave them from time to time on his tours through the Midwest. He got a lot of usage from them, and their popularity may be one reason that his wife let them be published in 1879, shortly after his death.

Studies in German Literature (1879)[31] consists of these lectures; they were collected by George Boker, who said that he left them unchanged. He cautions the reader that Taylor aimed at no more than introducing his audiences to German literature. Yet, such was "the native power of his intellect and the depth of his knowledge" that he developed an admirable style of treatment;[32] and Taylor's style in these lectures is clear, simple, and unpretentious.

In Taylor's first six lectures about early German literature, one sees that, though Taylor knew Goethe and contemporary authors quite well, he was not at home with the earlier material. Indeed, Krumpelmann offers considerable evidence that Taylor cribbed most of this early material from the work of the German scholar Heinrich Kurz. For example, Krumpelmann says of the first lecture that, "although the manuscript copy contains no notes indicative of sources, all the German selections embodied in this lecture are contained in the selected passages found in the Kurz text and have been appropriated *Seriatum.*"[33] Other sources are sometimes indicated, but it is plain that Taylor "was compelled to make quick acquaintance" with this material.

Nevertheless, such was Taylor's skill that he was able to make these early essays interesting to those who knew little of German literature. Taylor had the ability, from his journalistic experience, to pick out the salient features of material and to eliminate the rest. The best portions of these lectures are his translation of large swatches of poetry into reasonable English. He also spent much time on summary and historical background, and anyone who wants a brief survey of this material could do worse even today than read Taylor. Occasionally, he revealed an odd opinion such as that Luther's translation of the Bible is superior to the King James version because the "instinct of one great man" is better than the "average judgment of forty-seven men." But, for the most part, his opinions are not eccentric;

and he sees German literature as advancing steadily toward the expression of the people and away from the values of court life.

George Boker singles out the essays on Goethe, *Faust*, and Richter as the best; for these are "filled with the light of discovery, and . . . .with the most subtle and suggestive critical analysis." To these, Krumpelmann would add the lecture on Schiller; for, though it contains "little or nothing that is original or exceptional," it is the result of a "long familiarity with the life and works of that author."[34] These judgments are quite accurate.

Generally, Taylor's approach to a writer is to give a lengthy account of his life and career; then to describe his most important works, translating some passages to give the flavor; and, finally, to make a general judgment about the author's place in German literature. He is not devoted to analysis of text, but neither does he ignore the works themselves; indeed, his own strong interest in form makes him sound at times fairly modern. However, his criticism is likely to be intellectual—to center on the philosophical outlook of the author. Schiller, for example, had a "lofty, unceasing devotion to a noble literary Ideal." In his work, there was "an upward tendency—a lifting of the intellectual vision, a stirring as of unfolding wings. . . ." The highest rank cannot be awarded to Lessing "as a creative intellect"; but, as "a revolutionary power, as a shaping and organizing force, he has scarcely his equal in history."

For some years before his death, Taylor had been planning a combined biography of Goethe and Schiller. The two essays about these men are a foreshadowing of that interest, for they were in many ways bound together in Taylor's mind. The essay on Goethe is one of his best, and it succeeds in presenting Goethe (apart from his works) as a man of great variety and complexity. The essay on *Faust*, however, is somewhat disappointing in view of Taylor's great devotion to the poem. Of course, it is introductory; but his method is simply to summarize the story, with a running series of illustrative quotations from his own translation. This works fairly well, and the result is intelligent so far as the main lines of the poem are concerned; but one expects something more profound from a man who had devoted so much of his life to Goethe. Taylor's great contribution was, as has been noted earlier, his insistence on the integral relation of the second part to the whole; he argued that it completed and made meaningful the first part in a way that had not been appreciated. His statement of the essential meaning of the poem is this:

The first lesson is that man becomes morbid and miserable in seclusion, even though he devotes himself to the acquisition of knowledge. He must also know the life of the body in the open air, and the society of his fellow-men. . . .He must fight, through his life, with the powers of selfishness, doubt, denial of all good, truth and beauty. . . .The passion for the Beautiful must elevate and purify him, saving him from all the meanness and the littleness which we find in Society and in all forms of public life. The restless impulse, which drives him forward, will save him. . . .Only in constant activity and struggle can he redeem himself—Only in working for the benefit of his fellow-beings can he taste perfect happiness. This is the golden current of wisdom which flows through "Faust" from the beginning to end. (386-87)

Studies in German Literature is, on the whole, an interesting volume. As an introduction to the subject, it is informative, accurate, and well written. Taylor was attracted to German literature by certain qualities of his own mind; and the influence of the Germans, particularly Goethe, was very strong on him. His belief in constant striving (which might seem an American trait), his passion for "The Beautiful," his belief in a vigorous physicality, his love of society—these may well be partially derived from *Faust*. At any rate, his interest in German literature was genuine, though reinforced by his marriage and his German friendships. These essays show he was at ease in German literature, at least of the "classical" period; they suggest too, something of his importance in the field. According to Krumpelmann, he was "the foremost literary intermediary between this country and Germany."

IV *Other Criticism*

Critical Essays and Literary Notes (1883)[35] was a posthumous collection of miscellaneous pieces edited by Taylor's wife, who bemoaned the fact in her preface that he was forced to return, late in his career, to daily journalism at the *Tribune*. Most of the short pieces (some thirty-three of them) are from the Book Notes section of that paper, which he edited during his last few years; and they represent, she says, only a "minute proportion" of his work of this type. The volume also contains eight long essays drawn from journals like *The Atlantic Monthly* and *Scribner's* on literary topics—two of these are really travel pieces dealing with his researches on Goethe and Schiller.

The essay on Tennyson is the best, and it demonstrates that Taylor had considerable critical ability when he had time to exercise it. A fervent admirer of the poet, he was still able to make critical judgments about him. Tennyson's great virtues have been two: "an exquisitely luxurious sense of the charms of sound and rhythm" and "an earnest if not equal capacity for sober thought and reflection." Taylor thought Tennyson succeeded only partly in trying to perfect these powers; his early delight in sound led to an "over-anxiety" about unimportant details which, in turn, led to a kind of obscurity. Tennyson's devotion to his art had been excessive, with a general "over-refinement of the artistic sense." His chief shortcoming was intellectual, according to Taylor; "his dream of progress is a vague and shining mist, his view of the Present narrow and partisan." Nor had he "ventured beyond the common level of speculation, nor fore-spoken the deeper problems which shall engage the generation to come." Still, he was not morbid; his teaching has "always been wholesome and elevating." Indeed, Taylor expects a reaction against Tennyson in which public taste will undervalue his achievement; but his place will finally be high.

The essay on Victor Hugo was one of Taylor's most astonishing feats, and it was quoted far and wide as an example of what he could do. He received one evening two fat volumes (seven hundred and forty pages) of *La Légende des Siècles*, and by the following evening he had not only read it but had also written a review of eighteen pages, including translations of five long poems in the original meter. This feat is certainly impressive, though his wife's claim that it was "as much greater than the mechanical exploits of journalism as the spirit of man is superior to a machine" is rather doubtful. The accomplishment attests, instead, to the machine-like efficiency with which Taylor could work; and it also gives a clue about how he was able to produce such a tonnage of printed material.

A major portion of two essays on German authors, Friedrich Hebbel and Friedrich Rückert, is devoted to Taylor's translations of their poems. Those by Hebbel, "The German Burns," are of some interest for they are written in the Alemannic dialect, which Taylor tries to reproduce. Hebbel's poetry, he says, teaches a "wholesome morality"; but Taylor admits that this approach is not a legitimate one for judging them. Rückert, on the other hand, was a scholarly poet, known for his translations and imitations of Oriental poetry. Since Taylor had met him a few times, this essay is more biographical and personal.

"The Author of 'Saul'" deals with a Canadian, Charles Heavysege, a workingman who wrote verse dramas. Taylor speculates about talent versus environment as a producer of poets; he is on the side of talent—the "mute, inglorious Milton" is, he says, a "pleasant poetical fiction." But many quotations from the poem do not support Taylor's assertion that its language is "fresh, racy, vigorous" and that it "might have been written by a contemporary of Shakespeare." It is, in fact, a mediocre biblical drama.

The essay on Thackeray, written in 1864, consists mainly of personal reminiscences. The English novelist was "essentially manly" and had a "sadness of the moral sentiment which the world persisted in regarding as cynicism"; but his nature was "immoveably based on truth." Taylor's admiration for Thackeray is great; he speaks of him as "the man whom I honor as a master, while he gave me the right to love him as a friend."

Two long essays on Weimar, from 1875 to 1877, are mixtures of travel observation, comments on life in the city, and accounts of the difficulties Taylor had in gathering information about Goethe and Schiller. Because of Taylor's charm, he gained the confidence of those who had control over Goethe's house. And he was thrilled when recognized by a count or duke or invited to a court ball. At one point, when he gave a lecture on American literature in German, he discovered that American poets, such as Whittier, Stedman, Stoddard, and Aldrich, interested his audience.

The Notes section of the book opens with two addresses given for the dedication of monuments to Fitz-Greene Halleck, but in them Taylor makes some interesting comments about American literature. "The destiny that placed us on this soil," he says, as had many other Americans, "robbed us of the magic of tradition, the wealth of romance, the suggestions of history, the sentiment of inherited homes and customs, and left us ... to create a poetic literature for ourselves." Halleck himself was not important; he was genial and friendly, but his life "offers no enigmas for our solution." The monument symbolizes rather the "intellectual growth of the American people," and Halleck's life represents the "long period of transition between the appearance of American poetry and the creation of an appreciative audience for it."

In a review of Bryant's translation of the *Iliad*, Taylor repeats his own principles of translation, which have already been noted in his work on *Faust*. Though Bryant's translation doesn't always adhere to these principles, Taylor pronounces the translation very good, saying that blank verse will do until Americans become more accustomed to hexameters. Naturally, when comparing other translations of Homer, Taylor awards the palm to Bryant.

There are many short reviews of current books, sometimes by minor or obscure authors, and sometimes by his friends (who always get a good review; Stedman, for instance, is placed in the foremost rank of critics, beside Lowell and Matthew Arnold). When Taylor encounters a book of real merit, he is less certain; of George Eliot's *Daniel Deronda*, he says in a gingerly way that, when the crisis is reached in Eliot's novels and when her men and women "await a solution in which there shall be some ideal blending of the better possibilities of life, she closes her volume and turns away." This remark says more about Taylor than about Eliot, for he seems to desire an idealistic, or happy ending; yet he is able to see at least that her novels have substance and force.

The only other review of much interest today is of Henry James's *The American*, in which he complains that James is apparently untouched by sympathy for his characters. James habitually "gives us the various stages of a problem, and omits the solution." Taylor thinks Newman has utterly failed; and the only characters he cares for in the book are Valentin de Belle-garde and Mlle Noémie—all of which suggests that Taylor's comprehension of this novel was not total.

In short reviews like these an author cannot help appearing omniscient, and Taylor tends to fall into a pattern. He begins with comment on the author's life and career, makes a few remarks on his work generally, and then tries to fit the book into it, with occasional asides on art or poetry. Occasionally, Taylor indulges himself in wit, but he never attacks a book viciously.

For example, he says of the popular author "Ouida": ". . . With a pace which is meant to be that of a choric dance, but rather suggests the 'hop, skip and jump' of school-children, she circles around a mutilated altar, casting into the flame upon it huge handfuls of strange gums and spices, some of which give up a momentary sense of perfume, while others blind, strangle, and set us coughing." As reviews, they are above average for his day; for Taylor at least had standards which he applied with reasonable consistency.

Two closing essays on "Authorship in America" add little to what he has said before on this topic. On the one hand, he complains of the poor remuneration and the lack of official recognition; on the other, he insists that one writes for the joy of writing, not for profit. Of course, these views are not mutually exclusive; he simply means that a writer ought to be able to write without worrying about subsistence. But he concludes that it will be some time yet before this situation would be possible in the United States.

V *Juvenile Works*

Taylor turned his hand to almost anything that promised a fair return; and, in a few instances, he produced work for children. These are not remarkable but are usually at least competent. *The Ballad of Abraham Lincoln* (1870),[36] however, is an exception. Printed as a small eight-page pamphlet with garish illustrations by Sol Eytinge, Jr., and published by Fields in 1870, it is terrible. Fields, who had started a series to which Stoddard and Stedman made contributions, invited Taylor, who was inclined to contribute because he wasn't lecturing that year. The poem is extremely sentimental; furthermore, it is eighty-six stanzas long.

Another of Taylor's most disappointing projects was his *A School History of Germany* (1874).[37] He referred to it as a piece of hackwork he had undertaken because it would "kindle a better fire under the household pot than all my good work has done." But, after working at it steadily for months, he ran into difficulty with Appleton's, which was having trouble with illustrations. Time passed, publication was delayed several times, and Taylor's wife said he never received any remuneration from it at all. A substantial work of nearly six hundred pages, Taylor said that the history was "based" on three recent German works by Dittmar, Von Rochau, and Dr. David Muller; from these, he constructed "an entirely new narrative," compressing the material into less than half the space. This description reads more like abstracting than original writing, but Taylor claimed that his was the "only German history in existence, as a connected, unbroken narrative." Being without condescension or childishness, it seems well written for schools.

The book had a curious fate. Reprinted in 1897 with an additional chapter by Taylor's wife, it ultimately became part of a twenty-five volume set called The History of Nations, edited by Henry Cabot Lodge, which was published in 1907.[38] Taylor's volume was revised and reedited by Sidney B. Fay. According to Krumpelmann, the work went through twelve editions; thus, in a curious way it became one of Taylor's most successful works—though not one, as he had intended it, for children.

Boys of Other Countries (1876)[39] has received less attention than any of Taylor's books. The official biography, which mentions its publication, says that it consisted of a series of sketches published in *Our Young Folks* and in *St. Nicholas* magazines. Smyth, who says it was Taylor's last published prose book, calls it a "children's classic." The reasons for the lack of comment are two: the book is now hard to find, suggesting that it didn't sell very well; and, when found, there is little one can think of to say about it. It contains five stories: "The Little Post-Boy," about Sweden; "The Pasha's Son," about Khartoum; "Jon of Iceland," (for some reason three times longer than the others); "The Two Herd-Boys," about Germany; and "The Young Serf," about Russia. The tone is pleasantly informal, and the narrator is Taylor himself. The stories use his travel experiences, and they are not condescendingly written; indeed, they might be of interest to children even today. Another edition was published after Taylor's death, containing an additional story set in California.

Taylor produced hardly enough juvenilia for one to make generalizations about his talents as a writer for children. The Lincoln poem is terrible; the history, a compilation; and the short stories, moderately interesting. But all are examples of Taylor's versatility. He once made a clearcut distinction between his "professional" writing and his serious writing; these works clearly belong to the "professional" category.

Taylor's miscellaneous works constitute a large bulk of material, but much of it is unpublished. One might mention his lectures, for example, many of which are extant. There is also a large body of unreprinted periodical publication that might be delved into. An account of his many short translations would add little to one's assessment of him, nor would an account of his many lyrics that were set to music by various hands—"The Bedouin Song" no fewer than six different times. He also wrote introductions for several books by others; and, of course, he had an extensive correspondence with many people—thousands of his letters are extant in various libraries. But an account of this material would add little to what has already been said here— that he was an active and prolific journalist; a man of intelligence, taste, and skill who had to write for a living; and a writer who also wanted to be something more than a journalist—a literary man and a poet.

Conclusion

ON the sum of Taylor's writings, not very much, admittedly, is worth preserving; but some of it is—and not only for historical reasons. Of the travel books, *Eldorado* is lively and well written; both volumes of *At Home and Abroad* are particularly interesting for their American material; and parts of the other books are lively and curious. Of Taylor's fiction, *Hannah Thurston* deserves resuscitation, but some critics would no doubt argue for *The Story of Kennett*. *Poems of the Orient* deserves a modest place on the shelf of minor verse of that age, as well as a handful of the romances and lyrics; one might choose also some of the verse in *Prince Deukalion*. The parodies of *The Echo Club* should be better known; and, of course, the *Faust* translation occupies even today an honored place among the best translations of difficult poems. These works constitute a reasonable quantity of good work.

Still, Taylor remains for us a figure of more historical than literary interest. His great popularity may seem puzzling; it seemed at times puzzling to him, too, for he thought of himself as a "highbrow" literary man, not as a popular journalist. Yet his success is clearly due to several factors. One was a powerful ambition and drive; no man could have done all the things he did, or written all the books that he wrote, without enormous energy and a thirst for fame. In a sense, it is remarkable that he lived for fifty-three years.

Another factor of great importance in Taylor's success was the close-knit, almost incestuous, nature of the literary world in Taylor's time. He knew personally nearly everyone of importance, or someone who knew the people he didn't know. One can't help feeling at times that some of his material didn't deserve publication and that it wouldn't have been published in a more critical atmosphere. Reading Taylor's short stories, for example, one is moved to wonder how in the world they ever got published at all; but the same observation could be made of multi-

177

tudinous stories published in his era. The answer lies partly in his friendships with so many editors and literary men; for example, the editors of the *Atlantic Monthly* during the period Taylor published in it were James Russell Lowell (1857-1861); James T. Fields, Taylor's publisher (1861-1871); and William Dean Howells (1871-1881), with all of whom he was on friendly terms. Much the same was true of other periodicals to which he submitted material; it was seldom rejected, no matter how bad it may now seem. Therefore, he might be excused for thinking that his work was uniformly good.

But the third and perhaps most important reason for Taylor's success lies in the realm of taste, which, in mid-nineteenth-century America, was Genteel, in many ways reflecting English Victorianism. A central value of the Genteel tradition was an abstract ideal of beauty, one closely tied to an emphasis on purity and innocence and one usually symbolized by children and virgins. Of course, this emphasis ultimately derived from Christianity, which emphasized a clearly defined good and evil, chastity, asceticism, and so forth. Thus, the Genteel tradition's refusal to admit in literature the ugly and vulgar aspects of human existence suggests a kind of ascetic ideal. The tradition was not ignorant of crude reality; it simply chose to emphasize the perfection of an ideal. An etherealized woman, perfectly formed, was more to be tolerated than the animalistic possibilities of sex, childbirth, pain, and death.

But the values of the Genteel tradition were also essentially related to the upward mobility of the middle class. The values of money, hard work, and success—and its rewards, comfort and respectability—were all involved. They applied not only to the middle class, however, but also to those of the lower classes who aspired to rise. The price for this rise was very great, for it meant conformity to these principles, values, and attitudes. One accepted the proper values of reality, sex, marriage, family life, and of beauty, as well as the debt-paying conscience, the comfort, and the respect of society.

In a sense, Bayard Taylor was ruined by the Genteel tradition. He was a farmer's son who aspired to rise in society. This aspiration does not mean he lacked interest in literature; indeed, he was deeply absorbed in it, as it was understood by the Genteel. But the values of the tradition were those of wealth, comfort, and taste, which had no necessary relationship to literature, though the tradition could and did reward handsomely proper conformity to its principles. It is ironic to find Taylor so frequently condemning the public because he was conforming in fact to the Genteel public all the time. None of his work is very original or strikes out in new directions; he simply followed the forms, subjects, and themes of his time and of the era before him.

Obviously, there has been a fundamental change in taste between Taylor's time and the 1970's. Though some of the old views remain here and there in fragmentary form, the Genteel tradition was long ago routed not only in the sexual realm but also in regard to fundamental literary values. The literary life remains, and probably always will remain, an avenue of progress in society for poor boys with talent—as it should. Perhaps such persons still accept certain social values, but literary success now seems less dependent on social conventionality.

But the question of Bayard Taylor still nags at the mind. Would his work have been different in a different age? Why did he accept Genteel values so easily? Why couldn't he think his way through such superficiality toward some genuineness? Does his career mean that writers always reflect their age? Or is the only means one has of distinguishing between great writers and mediocre ones the fact that the great ones are intellectually free to rise above their age? The answers to these questions are not known; perhaps there are no answers to them; but this study of Taylor has tried to suggest some possibilities. On the other hand, the career of a minor author like Taylor—as well as those of his friends, too, Boker, Stedman, Stoddard, Aldrich—is interesting precisely because it is so typical of the age. In the last analysis, it is not their work which is interesting, but what it tells one about the taste of their age. In this sense, then, Taylor is important because he is typical of his age—its literary and social values—and because he embodies, both in his work and his person, the tenets of the Genteel tradition.

Notes and References

Chapter One

1. Albert H. Smyth, *Bayard Taylor,* American Men of Letters Series (Boston and New York, 1896), pp. 16-17.
2. *Ibid.,* p. 29.
3. *Ibid.,* p. 69.
4. John G. Whittier, *The Tent on the Beach and Other Poems* (Boston, 1868), p. 16.
5. According to the *Oxford English Dictionary,* ed. James A. H. Murray, *et. al.* (Oxford, 1933).
6. George Santayana's scattered writings about the Genteel Tradition have been conveniently collected recently by Douglas L. Wilson in *The Genteel Tradition: Nine Essays by George Santayana* (Cambridge, 1967).
7. R. H. Stoddard and Others, *Poets' Homes: Pen and Pencil Sketches of American Poets and their Homes* (Boston, 1879).
8. In *At Home and Abroad,* Second Series, 1862.
9. Marie Hansen-Taylor and Horace E. Scudder, eds., *Life and Letters of Bayard Taylor* (Boston, 1884), Vol. I, 367, 371.
10. *Ibid.,* I, 355.
11. *Ibid.,* II, 515.
12. *Ibid.,* II, 536.
13. *Ibid.,* II, 541.

Chapter Two

1. *Life and Letters,* I, 70.
2. *Views A-Foot; or, Europe seen with Knapsack and Staff* (New York, 1846). Page references are to a later edition by David McKay (Philadelphia, 1890).
3. In "Pilgrim's Return," *Literary History of the United States,* ed. Robert Spiller, *et. al.* (New York, 1959), p. 834.
4. *Ibid.,* 831.
5. *Ibid.*
6. *Eldorado; or, Adventures in the Path of Empire* (New York, 1850). Page references are to the centennial edition (New York, 1949) with an introduction by Robert Glass Cleland.
7. Cleland, *Ibid.,* p. vii.

8. John R. Schultz, ed., *The Unpublished Letters of Bayard Taylor in the Huntington Library* (San Marino, 1937), p. 22.

9. Richmond Croom Beatty, *Bayard Taylor: Laureate of the Gilded Age* (Norman, Oklahoma, 1936), p. 77.

10. *Life and Letters*, I, 149.

11. *A Journey to Central Africa, or Life and Landscapes from Egypt to the Negro Kingdoms of the White Nile* (New York, 1854). Page references here are to a later edition published by Putnam in 1875. However, Taylor purchased the plates of his travel books, and subsequent editions have the same pagination.

12. *Life and Letters*, I, 216.

13. *Ibid.*, I, 224.

14. *Ibid.*, I, 222.

15. *The Lands of the Saracen; or, Pictures of Palestine, Asia Minor, Sicily and Spain* (New York, 1854). Page references here are to an edition of 1855.

16. *Life and Letters*, I, 232-33.

17. *Ibid.*, I, 282.

18. *A Visit to India, China, and Japan in the Year 1853* (New York, 1855).

19. *Life and Letters*, I, 234.

20. *Ibid.*, I, 251.

21. *Ibid.*, I, 259.

22. *Ibid.*, I, 260.

23. *Ibid.*, I, 240.

24. *Cyclopaedia of Modern Travel* . . . (Cincinnati, 1856).

25. *Ibid.*, p. viii.

26. *Northern Travel. Summer and Winter Pictures. Sweden, Denmark and Lapland* (New York, 1857). Page references are to an edition of 1875.

27. *Life and Letters*, I, 327.

28. *Ibid.*, I, 314.

29. *Travels in Greece and Russia; With an Excursion to Crete* (New York, 1859). References here are to an edition of 1872.

30. Marie Hansen-Taylor (with the cooperation of Lilian Bayard Taylor Kiliani), *On Two Continents: Memories of Half a Century* (New York, 1905), pp. 50-51.

31. *Life and Letters*, I, 339.

32. *Ibid.*, I, 343.

33. *At Home and Abroad* (New York, 1859). References here are to an edition of 1867.

34. *At Home and Abroad*, Second Series (New York, 1862). References are to an edition of 1876.

35. *Life and Letters*, I, 355.

36. *Colorado: A Summer Trip* (New York, 1867).
37. *Life and Letters*, I, 384.
38. Schultz, *op. cit.*, p. 91.
39. *Ibid.*, p. 94.
40. *By-Ways of Europe* (New York, 1869).
41. *Life and Letters*, II, 469.
42. *Ibid.*, II, 474.
43. *Ibid.*, II, 472.
44. *Ibid.*, II, 482.
45. *Egypt and Iceland in the Year 1874* (New York, 1874).
46. *Life and Letters*, II, 527.
47. *Ibid.*, II, 529.
48. *Ibid.*, II, 601.

Chapter Three

1. All books published by G. P. Putnam & Son, New York.
 2. Smyth, pp. 157-58.
 3. *Life and Letters*, II, 453.
 4. Quoted in *Life and Letters*, II, 417.
 5. *Ibid.*, II, 417.
 6. *Ibid.*
 7. Smyth, p. 163.
 8. *Life and Letters*, II, 451.
 9. *Ibid.*
10. Smyth, p. 165.
11. *Life and Letters*, II, 453.
12. *Ibid.*, II, 457.
13. *Ibid.*
14. Smyth, p. 168.
15. Beatty, p. 240.
16. *Life and Letters*, II, 465-66.
17. *On Two Continents*, pp. 161-62.
18. Smyth, p. 175.
19. *Ibid.*, p. 177.
20. *Life and Letters*, II, 552.
21. *Ibid.*, I, 372.
22. *Ibid.*
23. *On Two Continents*, p. 134.

Chapter Four

1. From "Proem Dedicatory" to *Poems of the Orient*; "An Epistle from Mount Tmolus," ll. 13-15.
 2. From "Porphyrogenitus," ll. 1-2.

3. Quoted in *Life and Letters,* I, 21; Stanza 2 of nine.

4. *Ximena, or the Battle of Sierra Morena* (Philadelphia, 1844). Later suppressed by Taylor, this volume is very rare.

5. *Life and Letters,* I, 31.

6. Smyth, p. 32.

7. R. H. Stoddard, *Recollections, Personal and Literary* (New York, 1903), p. 58.

8. Smyth, p. 33.

9. E. C. Stedman, *Poets of America* (Boston & New York, 1893), p. 400.

10. *Rhymes of Travel, Ballads and Poems* (New York, 1849).

11. The Poe opinion is reported by Smyth, p. 216, and by Stedman, p. 402.

12. Stedman, p. 402.

13. *Life and Letters,* I, 138.

14. *A Book of Romances, Lyrics and Songs* (Boston, 1851).

15. *Life and Letters,* I, 212.

16. Quoted in Beatty, p. 110.

17. Smyth, p. 217.

18. W. S. Tryon and Wm. Charvat, eds., *The Cost Books of Ticknor and Fields* (New York, 1950).

19. *Poems of the Orient* (Boston, 1854).

20. Smyth, pp. 218-19.

21. Stedman, p. 408.

22. *Life and Letters,* I, 296.

23. Beatty, p. 172.

24. "Proem Dedicatory," Stanza IV, ll. 1-9.

25. Smyth, p. 177.

26. Smyth, p. 220. Essentially repeated in his introduction to *The Poems of Bayard Taylor* (New York, 1907).

27. Smyth, p. 222.

28. *Poems of Home and Travel* (Boston, 1855).

29. *The Poet's Journal* (Boston, 1862).

30. *Life and Letters,* I, 367.

31. *Ibid.,* I, 371.

32. *Ibid.,* I, 404.

33. Stedman, p. 419.

34. Smyth, pp. 224-25.

35. *Life and Letters,* I, 405.

36. *The Picture of St. John* (Boston, 1866).

37. *Life and Letters,* II, 442-43.

38. Quoted in Beatty, p. 244.

39. John T. Krumpelmann, *Bayard Taylor and German Letters* (Hamburg, 1959), p. 104.

40. Beatty, p. 248.
41. *Ibid.*, II, 467.
42. *Life and Letters,* II. Longfellow, Lowell, Bryant, p. 467; Holmes, Whittier, p. 468.
43. Beatty, p. 248.
44. *Ibid.,* pp. 247-48.
45. Smyth, p. 230.
46. Beatty, p. 248.
47. (Boston, 1872).
48. *Life and Letters,* II, 572.
49. *Ibid.,* II, 575.
50. Charles Duffy, ed., *The Correspondence of Bayard Taylor and Paul Hamilton Hayne* (Baton Rouge, 1945), p. 52.
51. *Life and Letters,* II, 592.
52. *Lars: A Pastoral of Norway* (Boston, 1873). Page references here are to *The Poetical Works of Bayard Taylor* (New York, 1892).
53. *Life and Letters,* II, 621.
54. Stedman, pp. 425-26.
55. Beatty, p. 327.
56. *Life and Letters,* II, 631.
57. *On Two Continents,* p. 255.
58. *Ibid.*
59. *Life and Letters,* II, 661.
60. *The Prophet: A Tragedy* (Boston, 1874).
61. *Life and Letters,* II, 647.
62. *Ibid.,* II, 665.
63. *Home Pastorals, Ballads and Lyrics* (Boston, 1875).
64. *Life and Letters,* II, 517.
65. *The National Ode* (Boston, 1877).
66. *Life and Letters,* I, 189.
67. *Ibid.,* II, 586.
68. *Ibid.,* II, 687.
69. Stedman, p. 427.
70. Beatty, p. 344.
71. Quoted in Beatty, p. 344.
72. *Life and Letters,* II, 677.
73. *Prince Deukalion* (Boston, 1878).
74. Smyth, p. 258.
75. Beatty, p. 349.
76. *Life and Letters,* II, 764.
77. Krumpelmann, p. 122.
78. Willard Thorp, "Defenders of Ideality," *Literary History of The United States* (New York, 1959), p. 822.
79. Duffy, *op. cit.,* p. 99.

80. *The Poetical Works,* and *The Dramatic Works* (Boston and New York, 1880).

81. *Ibid.,* p. iv.

82. *Ibid.*

Chapter Five

1. *Faust, A Tragedy,* by Johann Wolfgang von Goethe, translated in the original meters, by Bayard Taylor. Part I (Boston, 1870); Part II (Boston, 1871). References here are to the one-volume edition published by Houghton, Mifflin and Company (successors to Fields and Osgood) in 1900.

2. *Life and Letters,* II, 542.

3. *Ibid.,* II, 544.

4. *Ibid.,* II, 545.

5. *Ibid.,* II, 540.

6. Krumpelmann, p. 53.

7. A photocopy of this review, which was set in type, is also in the Yale University library.

8. Pp. 443 and 444 of the type-set copy.

9. Schultz, pp. 153-54.

10. *Ibid.,* p. 156.

11. Haskell, *Bayard Taylor's Translation of Goethe's Faust* (New York, 1908).

12. Preface to *Faust,* pp. xiv-xv.

13. *Ibid.,* p. viii.

14. Haskell, p. 34.

15. *Ibid.,* p. 83.

16. Krumpelmann, p. 177, note 170.

17. Spiller, ed., *Literary History of the United States,* p. 823.

18. Beatty, p. 280. On the other hand, Carl Van Doren, in the *Dictionary of American Biography,* said: "Its fidelity and sonorousness should not be allowed to hide the fact that Taylor rendered *Faust* in the second-rate English poetry which was all he knew how to write."

19. Krumpelmann, p. 54.

20. *Ibid.,* p. 55.

21. *Ibid.,* p. 46.

22. *Ibid.,* pp. 215-21.

23. *Ibid.,* p. 61. See also p. 166, note 4, to "Introduction."

24. (Boston, 1876).

25. *Life and Letters,* II, 566.

26. Beatty, pp. 257-58.

27. *Life and Letters,* II, 620.

28. W. P. Trent, *History of American Literature* (New York, 1903), p. 470; quoted in Haskell, p. 13.

29. In the *Atlantic Monthly* (January, 1877), quoted by Haskell, p. 13.

30. Haskell, p. 14.

31. *Studies in German Literature* (New York, 1879).

32. Introduction to *Studies in German Literature,* p. v.

33. Krumpelmann, p. 145.

34. *Ibid.,* p. 142.

35. *Critical Essays and Literary Notes* (New York, 1880).

36. *The Ballad of Abraham Lincoln,* Illustrated (Boston, 1870).

37. *A School History of Germany: From the Earliest Period to the Establishment of the German Empire in 1871* (New York, 1874).

38. *Germany* (Vol. 18 of *The History of Nations,* Henry Cabot Lodge, editor-in-chief), revised and edited from the work of Bayard Taylor by Sidney B. Fay (Chicago, Copyright 1907 by John D. Morris & Co.; Copyright 1910 by the H. W. Snow Co.).

39. *Boys of Other Countries. Stories for American Boys* (New York, 1876).

Selected Bibliography

PRIMARY SOURCES

(The order is chronological within groups. Edited works are marked (Ed.). The list does not include editions subsequent to the first; foreign editions; works for which Taylor wrote a preface; or a few poems published individually.)

1. *Travel Works*

Views A-Foot; or Europe seen with Knapsack and Staff. New York: Wiley & Putnam, 1846.

Eldorado, or, Adventures in the Path of Empire. Comprising a Voyage to California, via Panama; Life in San Francisco and Monterey; Pictures of the Gold Region, and Experiences of Mexican Travel. New York: George P. Putnam, 1850.

A Journey to Central Africa, or Life and Landscapes from Egypt to the Negro Kingdoms of the White Nile. New York: G. P. Putnam & Co., 1854.

The Lands of the Saracen; or Pictures of Palestine, Asia Minor, Sicily and Spain. New York: G. P. Putnam & Co., 1854.

A Visit to India, China, and Japan in the Year 1853. New York: G. P. Putnam & Co., 1855.

(Ed.) *Cyclopaedia of Modern Travel.* Cincinnati: Moore, Willstach, Keys & Co., 1856.

Northern Travel. Summer and Winter Pictures. Sweden, Denmark and Lapland. New York: G. P. Putnam, 1857.

Travels in Greece and Russia, with an Excursion to Crete. New York: G. P. Putnam, 1859.

At Home and Abroad: A Sketch-Book of Life, Scenery and Men. New York: G. P. Putnam, 1859.

At Home and Abroad, Second Series. New York: G. P. Putnam, 1862.

Colorado: A Summer Trip. New York: G. P. Putnam, 1867.

By-Ways of Europe. New York: G. P. Putnam, 1869.

(Ed.) *Travels in Arabia.* New York: Charles Scribner's Sons, 1871.

(Ed.) *Japan in Our Day.* New York: Charles Scribner's Sons, 1872.

(Ed.) *Travels in South Africa.* New York: Charles Scribner's Sons, 1872.

189

(Ed.) *The Lake Regions of Central Africa.* New York: Charles
    Scribner's Sons, 1873.
Egypt and Iceland in the Year 1874. New York: G. P. Putnam's
    Sons, 1874.
(Ed.) *Central Asia, Travels in Cashmere, Little Thibet and Central
    Asia.* New York: Charles Scribner's Sons, 1874.
(Ed.) *Picturesque Europe: Delineations by Pen and Pencil of the
    Natural Features and the Picturesque and Historical Places of
    Great Britain and the Continent.* New York: D. Appleton &
    Co., 1877.

2. *Fiction*

Hannah Thurston, A Story of American Life. New York: G. P. Put-
    nam, 1863.
*John Godfrey's Fortunes: Related by Himself. A Story of American
    Life.* New York: G. P. Putnam, 1864.
The Story of Kennett. New York: G. P. Putnam, 1866.
Joseph and His Friend. New York: G. P. Putnam, 1870.
Beauty and the Beast, and Tales of Home. New York: G. P. Putnam
    & Sons, 1872.

3. *Poetry*

Ximena, or the Battle of the Sierra Morena, and Other Poems. Phila-
    delphia: Herman Hooker, 1844.
Rhymes of Travel, Ballads and Poems. New York: George P. Putnam,
    1849.
A Book of Romances, Lyrics and Songs: Boston: Ticknor, Reed and
    Fields, 1851.
Poems of the Orient. Boston: Ticknor and Fields, 1854.
Poems of Home and Travel. Boston: Ticknor and Fields, 1855.
The Poet's Journal. Boston: Ticknor and Fields, 1862.
The Poems of Bayard Taylor. Blue and Gold edition. Boston: Ticknor
    and Fields, 1864.
The Poems of Bayard Taylor. Cabinet edition. Boston: Ticknor and
    Fields, 1865.
The Picture of St. John. Boston: Fields, Osgood & Co., 1866.
The Golden Wedding: A Masque. Philadelphia: J. B. Lippincott &
    Co., 1868.
The Ballad of Abraham Lincoln. Boston: Fields, Osgood & Co., 1870.
The Masque of the Gods. Boston: James R. Osgood & Co., 1872.
Lars: A Pastoral of Norway. Boston: James R. Osgood & Co., 1873.
The Prophet. A Tragedy. Boston: James R. Osgood & Co., 1874.

Home Pastorals, Ballads and Lyrics. Boston: James R. Osgood & Co., 1875.
The National Ode. Boston: William F. Gill & Co., 1877.
Prince Deukalion, A Lyrical Drama. Boston: Houghton, Osgood & Co., 1878.
Poetical Works of Bayard Taylor. Household edition. Boston: Houghton, Osgood and Co., 1880.
Dramatic Works of Bayard Taylor. Boston: Houghton, Mifflin & Co., 1880.

4. *Critical and Other Works*

(Ed.) *Hand-book of Literature and Fine Arts.* New York: George P. Putnam & Co., 1852.
Faust, A Tragedy, by Johann Wolfgang von Goethe. Part I. Boston: Fields, Osgood & Co., 1870.
Faust, A Tragedy, by Johann Wolfgang von Goethe. Part II. Boston: James R. Osgood & Co., 1871.
A School History of Germany: from the Earliest Period to the Establishment of the German Empire in 1871. New York: D. Appleton & Co., 1874.
The Echo Club and other Literary Diversions. Boston: J. R. Osgood & Co., 1876.
Boys of Other Countries: Stories for American Boys. New York: G. P. Putnam's Sons, 1876.
Studies in German Literature. New York: G. P. Putnam's Sons, 1879.
Critical Essays and Literary Notes. New York: G. P. Putnam's Sons, 1880.

5. *Manuscript Materials*

Taylor's manuscripts and letters are scattered throughout several libraries, but the largest collections are at Cornell and Harvard. There are also collections, however, at West Chester Historical Museum and Library, The Huntington Library, The New York Public Library, The University of Pennsylvania Library, and Yale University Library. Published works drawn from this material:

CARY, RICHARD. *The Genteel Circle: Bayard Taylor and His New York Friends.* Ithaca: Cornell University Press, 1952. Half of this pamphlet consists of letters from Taylor to Stoddard, Stedman, and Aldrich. The rest is a perceptive account of the Genteel Tradition.
DUFFY, CHARLES, ed. *The Correspondence of Bayard Taylor and Paul Hamilton Hayne.* Baton Rouge: Louisiana State University Press,

1945. Twenty-seven by Hayne; nineteen by Taylor. Hayne seems
groveling; Taylor is cheerful, harassed, big-brotherish.

LANIER, H. W., ed. "Letters between Two Poets: The Correspondence
of Bayard Taylor and Sidney Lanier." *Atlantic Monthly,* LXXXIII
(1899), 791-807; LXXXIV (1899), 127-41. More from Lanier
than Taylor. Lanier is respectful, admiring; Taylor is helpful
but harassed. Much about poetic problems.

PRAHL, A. J. "Bayard Taylor's Letters from Russia," *Huntington
Library Quarterly,* IX (1946), 411-18. Information about a
little-known period of Taylor's career.

SCHULTZ, JOHN R., ed. *The Unpublished Letters of Bayard Taylor
in the Huntington Library.* San Marino, 1937. Very useful
volume; reprints or summarizes all the Taylor letters in the
Huntington.

WARNOCK, ROBERT. "Bayard Taylor's Unpublished Letters to his
Sister Annie," *American Literature,* VII (1935), 47-55. An
account of one hundred twenty-one letters in a private collection.
Useful about expense of building "Cedarcroft."

———. "Unpublished Lectures of Bayard Taylor," *American Literature,* V (1933), 123-32. Accounts of the ideas and subjects of
fourteen lectures in the West Chester library.

SECONDARY SOURCES

BEATTY, RICHMOND CROOM. *Bayard Taylor: Laureate of the Gilded
Age.* Norman: University of Oklahoma Press, 1936. Most recent
estimate of Taylor; sees him as a victim of American life. Many
inaccuracies; has a Southern bias.

CONWELL, RUSSELL H. *The Life, Travels, and Literary Career of
Bayard Taylor.* Boston: B. B. Russell & Co., 1879. Generally
considered hackwork; depends heavily on the travel books.

HANSEN-TAYLOR, MARIE, and HORACE E. SCUDDER, eds. *Life and
Letters of Bayard Taylor.* 2 vols. Boston: Houghton, Mifflin and
Company, 1884. A standard type, much of this consists of Tay-
lor's letters; still a valuable source, despite tone of hallowed piety.

HANSEN-TAYLOR, MARIE, with the cooperation of LILIAN BAYARD
TAYLOR KILIANI. *On Two Continents: Memories of Half a Century.* New York: Doubleday, Page & Company, 1905. Mrs.
Taylor's life with a great poet; reproduces some of Taylor's
paintings.

SMYTH, ALBERT H. *Bayard Taylor.* American Men of Letters Series.
Boston and New York: Houghton, Mifflin and Co., 1896. Still
a good piece of work, accurate and honest, though permeated
to a degree by Genteel values. Has valuable bibliographies.

Van Doren, Carl. "Bayard Taylor." *Dictionary of American Biography*. New York: C. Scribner's Sons, 1943-1958. An intelligent short account, this may stand as representative of many others.

Many brief accounts of Taylor's life and works may be found in early histories of American literature, journals, magazines, and memoirs until about the turn of the century. Most are sketchy (Horace Greeley's *Recollections of a Busy Life* [New York, 1868] devotes exactly one paragraph to Taylor), and all tend to say the same things. A thorough listing of such sources, and of reviews of Taylor's books, can be found in Haskell (see below). In addition, a lengthy list covering Taylor's German interests can be found in Krumpelmann (listed below). Therefore, I list here only those works I have referred to, quoted from, or found valuable in some way.

Bradley, Scully. "Pilgrim's Return." *Literary History of the United States*. New York: The Macmillan Company, 1959. Interesting comments on American travel works.
————. *George Henry Boker: Poet and Patriot*. Philadelphia: University of Pennsylvania Press, 1927. Interesting life of one of Taylor's close (and rich) friends.
Branch, Douglas. *The Sentimental Years, 1836-1860*. New York: D. Appleton-Century Company, Inc., 1934. Good background reading about the world of *John Godfrey*.
Flanagan, John T. "Bayard Taylor's Minnesota Visits," *Minnesota History*, XIX (1938), 399-418.
Frenz, Horst. "Bayard Taylor and the Reception of Goethe in America," *Journal of English and Germanic Philology*, XLI (1942), 121-39. Taylor as intermediary between America and Germany.
———— and P. A. Shelley. "Bayard Taylor's German Lecture on American Literature," *Jahrbuch für Amerikastudien*, II (1957), 89-133.
Greenslet, Ferris. *The Life of Thomas Bailey Aldrich*. Boston: Houghton Mifflin Company, 1908. Another of Taylor's friends.
Haskell, Juliana. *Bayard Taylor's Translation of Goethe's Faust*. New York: Columbia University Press, 1908. Presents the case against Taylor's *Faust* as a great translation.
Howells, William Dean. *Literary Friends and Acquaintance*. New York: Harper and Brothers, 1900. A somewhat adulatory account of the New England worthies in literature.
Krumpelmann, John T. *Bayard Taylor and German Letters*. Hamburg: Cram, de Gruyter & Co., 1959. Most thorough account of Taylor's German interests.

LIEDER, F. W. C. "Bayard Taylor's Adaptation of Schiller's Don
    Carlos," *Journal of English and Germanic Philology*, XVI (1917),
    27-52. Description of a work no longer available.
MABIE, H. W. "Bayard Taylor: Adventurer," *Bookman*, XLIII (1916),
    51-59.
PRAHL, A. J. "Bayard Taylor and Goethe," *Modern Language Quar-
    terly*, VII (1946), 205-17.
SANTAYANA, GEORGE. *Character and Opinion in the United States*.
    New York: Charles Scribner's Sons, 1920. Fascinating analysis
    of the Genteel Tradition by the man who invented the term.
SHELLEY, PHILIP A. "Bayard Taylor and Schiller's Don Carlos,"
    Crosscurrents, 13 (1962), 33-96.
SMYTH, ALBERT H. *The Poems of Bayard Taylor*. New York: Thomas
    Y. Crowell Co., 1907. Intelligent selection of Taylor's best verse.
STEDMAN, E. C. *Poets of America*. Boston and New York: Houghton,
    Mifflin and Company, 1885. Interesting judgments by a close
    friend.
STODDARD, R. H. *Recollections, Personal and Literary*. New York:
    Barnes, 1903. One of Taylor's good friends is surprisingly ob-
    jective about him.
————— and OTHERS. *Poets' Homes: Pen and Pencil Sketches of
    American Poets and their Homes*. Boston: D. Lothrop Co., 1879.
    How Genteel poets lived, including Taylor.
TRYON, W. S. *Parnassus Corner: A Life of James T. Fields*. Boston:
    Houghton, Mifflin Company, 1964. Useful insights into nine-
    teenth-century publishing.
————— and WILLIAM CHARVAT. *The Cost Books of Ticknor and
    Fields*. New York: The Bibliographical Society, 1950. Details
    of edition sizes, costs, royalties, and so forth.
WHITTIER, JOHN G. *The Tent on the Beach and Other Poems*. Boston:
    Ticknor and Fields, 1868. Volume dedicated to Taylor.
WILSON, DOUGLAS L., ed. *The Genteel Tradition, Nine Essays by
    George Santayana*. Cambridge: Harvard University Press, 1967.
WILSON, JAMES G. *Bryant and His Friends*. New York: G. P. Put-
    nam, 1886.
WINTER, WILLIAM. *Old Friends, Being Literary Recollections of
    Other Days*. New York: Moffat, Yard & Co., 1909.
WOODBERRY, G. E. *Literary Memoirs of the Nineteenth Century*. New
    York: Harcourt, Brace and Co., 1921.

Index